1991

MW01045157

SunRise Tomorrow

SunRise Tomorrow

ELIZABETH B. BROWN

FLEMING H. REVELL COMPANY
OLD TAPPAN, NEW JERSEY

Library of Congress Cataloging-in-Publication Data

Brown, Betty B.
   Sunrise Tomorrow / Elizabeth B. Brown.
      p.   cm.
   Bibliography: p.
   ISBN 0-8007-1576-4
   1. Bereavement—Psychological aspects.   2. Children—Death—
Psychological aspects.   3. Parent and child.   4. Brown. Betty B.—
Family.   5. Mothers—United States—Biography.   I. Title.
BF575.G7B755 1988
155.9'37—dc 19   87-28599
                                                                           CIP

Copyright © 1988 by Elizabeth B. Brown
Published by the Fleming H. Revell Company
Old Tappan, New Jersey   07675
Printed in the United States of America

To my husband, Paul,
who as we have walked together through the
high times and the low times
has become my true love
and
Kim, Paul, LeeAnne, and Brad,
who have given meaning to the word
joy.

Contents

Preface

This book is written to you—a straight, no-holds-barred conversation about death. If you hurt from the loss of your child, these guides may help you put your life back together. If you are a friend of someone who has lost a child, you will find understanding and ways to support and uphold the griever.

If you have a child whose friend has died, you face one of life's most difficult challenges, because the way you handle your child's grief will influence him throughout his years. You must understand the crucial needs of a child discussed here.

But I suppose that most who read this book are parents, parents like Paul and me, who have lost their dearest treasure. As the parents of the deceased child, your family unit is in danger of being swallowed by the tragedy. You must confront and jump the hurdles that come with your child's death. Failure means your family will face the dangers of divorce, severe depression, and inability to cope with life.

Sunrise Tomorrow deals with the stunning harshness of our child's death. But more than that, it is a story of shock, grief, and finally renewed hope. It is a story of survival.

SunRise Tomorrow

One

Are We Alone? _____

Let go. You have to let LeeAnne go, Betty. The pain won't stop until you release her. The words echoed between my silent screams. *Never! It is not possible to let go. Memories are all I have. If I turn her loose, she will be gone. My little girl will be gone. . . .*

My child is dead. My precious bubble of enthusiasm who made me feel needed and loved has been laid in a pretty, white casket. She is alone. They put her in a hole in the ground. That is no place for a little girl. She is going to be afraid. She needs her mommy.

The pain is so intense. Someone is dragging a knife through me, gouging me, turning it. No! It isn't a knife. It is a scream. A scream tears my body apart, pushing, penetrating. It fills my head until a low wail escapes. Convulsive heaves change to dry, wrenching vomiting. I feel tired, dull, lifeless. The silence is crashing like thunder. The scream is beginning again.

Sleep is gone. The endless nights are filled with fragmented thoughts, questions, wet pillowcases. Paul and I cling together, holding each other. His quiet sobs alternate with mine. The emptiness is a black hole that sucks our strength, consumes our emotions. It eats more voraciously in the stillness.

Is this just a dream? No. Dreams are not like this. Nightmares are not like this. They end. Tonight I relive choosing an outfit for Lee's burial—for the thousandth time. The thoughts are like a McDonald's sign—*We sold 1 million hamburgers, 2 million. . . .* I pick out the treasured purple, long dress with the pink sash, little crocheted socks with flowers. She wore that special dress to school, to church, to be a fairy princess. I add her soft Care Bear with the big heart. She would want something to cuddle. The sick feeling that filled my stomach when we left the dress at the funeral home begins again. Tonight makes 1,001. God, I can't stand this! *Why didn't You save our little girl?* I want her. . . .

Children Do Die

We are alone, alone in the world. Children don't die. I mean real children, children who have been born and leave the hospital. I don't know anyone whose child died. No one looks at us. Everyone looks down or to the side. They know children don't die. They know! I know! . . .

But, children do die. Every year in America 100,000

children under the age of twenty-four die from catastrophic illness, accident, suicide, or murder. One in every 350 infants dies before his or her first birthday, 48,000 deaths per year.[1] Sudden Infant Death Syndrome is responsible for 7,000 infant deaths yearly.[2] In addition every year 32,000 babies die in the womb of mothers who excitedly awaited their baby's birth.[3]

Suicide is the sixth leading cause of death in children between ages five and fifteen; the second leading cause between ages fifteen and twenty-four, accounting for 5,200 yearly deaths. From accidents, twenty-six children die a day—more than one an hour, nearly 10,000 a year. Almost 2,500 deaths would be added to the toll if we counted only 10 percent of the sixty-three violence-related deaths per day. Unfortunately, with the 200 percent increase in child abuse during the past decade, the booming child pornography and prostitution market, 10 percent is considered underreporting.[4]

So, it is a myth that children do not die! Children do die! When your child dies, you are not alone. You are not the only person to have to survive such a tragedy. You, like the others, will survive—if you choose to.

This book is a guideline to survival. When your child dies, the hurt is so great, it does not seem possible to go on living. Part of you has been severed, cut off, and the wound is bleeding. Nothing functions the same. The mind seems to be shut down, foggy, disorganized, disoriented. The emotions are brittle. Tears fall constantly, unexpectedly. Sleep is impossible. The body is weak, uninterested in activity or food, susceptible to every virus. Katherine Fair Donnelly commented, "The early days of grief are a period no parent gets through. It's just an existence of nonexistence and anguish. The beginning of survival comes much later."[5]

However, from the first day your child is deceased, you must consciously begin to make decisions to live. You must choose to survive, for if you fail to make the conscious decision, you and your family will fall apart. Here are the dangers: Half of those who lose a child report serious health problems within two years; 35 percent are under psychiatric care; 25 percent report psychosomatic disorders such as ulcers, colitis, or hypertension in a family member; 40 percent have a serious drinking or drug problem; 48 percent have at least one child with serious school problems; 43 percent report significant difficulty in the mother's homemaking ability; 88 percent feel a family member to be abnormally consumed with morbid grief reactions.[6]

Does it make a difference if parents had longtime knowledge of a child's pending death, such as in cases of leukemia? No! In his study of such families, Dr. Charles Kaplan found most parents cling desperately to the hope their child will be spared; they do not deal with the possibility of their own child's death.

Among the few parents who realistically faced the death possibility, Kaplan found a significant difference in coping actions. They did not try to evade, deny, wish away, or use drugs to blank out their intense emotions. They analyzed their family situation and designed an escape route from grieving to living.

To take control, you must understand what is involved in grieving. You must learn about the emotions, so you can control them, and know the stages a griever passes through. As you become aware of the dangers and pitfalls, you can help walk your family around the traps. However, if you fail to fight for survival, the pain will never go away. Your life will become an endless struggle with resentment and anger; and happiness will become a vague memory. The life that ended will become the vortex of the entire family's demise.

Routes to survival involve reason and the knowledge of God's love and God-given directions. At a time when the emotions want to have full control, you must deal with the reality of your loss from a base of reason.

Successful survival will be the most difficult task of your life. Look at your options: Either you make it, whole and filled with God's love, new insights, and even tighter family bonds; or you fail, bringing down your marriage, children, and all other relationships. Obviously, you want to survive. It won't be easy, but with God's help and the gradual ability to "let go" of what once was, you will be whole again.

People who move more rapidly through the grief process:

1. Accept the reality of the child's death.
2. Stop wishing for what used to be.
3. Agree to let life continue.
4. Take control of their lives, not allowing their emotions of grief to be in control.

So easy to say, "Let go!" "Accept the death." "Go on with life." So difficult to do!

Two

Why Me, Lord? _____

I refuse to listen. I hear every word, but I refuse to listen. She will not die. The doctors do not know. She can live. They know all the bad, the extreme, the rare. Children are resilient. She will make it. We will not "let" her go.

The nurses are so quiet, so concerned. I read their every glance. They are ever-busy, checking this, plugging in that, monitoring, moving, never looking directly at me.

Friday we were planning her birthday party. Today, three days later, she lies plugged into machines to breathe, monitor, and feed, a screw in her head, no signs of brain activity. The weekend had been quiet, with our watching Lee's flulike illness. Something was wrong, but there were no vital signs askew. Then the dream began with Paul frantically dressing as I tucked LeeAnne into a blanket, to ward off early-morning cold in the car. Paul wanted verification that all was still well. No outward signs indicated any danger—just an ominous feeling.

After taking our sixteen-year-old son, Paul Edward, to high school and our two-year-old son, Brad, to the baby-sitter, I drive to the hospital. There is no panic. LeeAnne had been in the hospital several times. Paul is there. No one would take care of her better than her daddy, who is also a doctor. But when I enter her hall, there is an unusual quietness. There is no nurse on the wing. Her room is empty, not even a bed. With sudden awareness, I know.

I can't breathe. The gulps of air drown me. I have to stay calm. Maybe I am going to pass out. My imagination is going crazy. There is nothing wrong, except I feel it. *Please, please, someone come find me. Tell me I do not feel death. I can't move.*

LeeAnne has talked to the specialists around her bed, shared with them her four puppies' names, talked about her baby brother. She is lethargic, but mentally alert. There are no neurological indications of anything wrong. Just wait, watch, and take more tests. Then, as Paul lifts her back into the hospital bed, her head drops, pupils dilate, and she dies in his arms. There is no way to describe the sheer terror, then the numbness.

In seconds the team wheels her into intensive care, restarts her heart, plugs her into every available monitor, and puts a screw into her head to relieve pressure. It looks like Reye's syndrome, insidious, quiet, deadly.

But she is alive again. The respirator fills her lungs with air. Her heart is moving. She is a fighter. She hasn't finished her purpose here on earth. This is a hurdle. We will beat the problem. It will take time to get her strength back . . . maybe we can have the birthday party in two weeks!

Understanding the Stages

Most people recognize that there are stages to grief. We can not deal with the full reality of tragedy instantly. It must be absorbed slowly.

Elisabeth Kübler-Ross, the world's foremost authority on the stages of death and dying, divides the grief process into five steps:

BARGAINING: Period before death, when family members plead with God.

DENIAL: Avoidance technique, which functions as a buffer after the death and allows the survivor to collect himself and mobilize less radical defenses.

ANGER: Out-of-control rage, envy, and resentment reign over the emotions.

DEPRESSION: Sense of great loss, drained emotions, and hopelessness replace anger.

ACCEPTANCE: Void of feeling which moves toward reentry into normal roles of life.[1]

Charles Gerkin in *Crisis Experience in Modern Life* describes four progressions:

Shock, often accompanied by denial of the reality; overwhelming feelings of impending loss, numbness.

Emerging awareness of the threat of disintegration of self; often accompanied by thoughts of suicide, fears about the possibility of terminal illness, death wishes, and intense guilt.

Idealization of the lost relationship; move toward making that

relationship the ultimate one in the bereaved person's life.
Discovering meaning in new relationships and experiences; awareness that the self has not disintegrated.[2]

In the book *Normal and Pathological Responses to Bereavement*, John Bowlby and Murray Parkes, British psychologists who pioneered much of the research in bereavement, divide grief into four stages.

Numbness: Reality of the loss is considered.
Yearning: Desire to recover the loss predominates; searching takes place.
Disorganization: Loss is accepted and attempts to recover the loss are given up.
Reorganization of behavior.[3]

Common Denominators

These approaches to understanding and staging have a common denominator: They recognize that the mind moves in predictable steps to reorganize after the loss of a loved one. The fact that the process is laborious highlights the interwoven threads that bind us together. When a child dies, we not only lose a precious baby, but part of our hearts dies. We are left with holes in our souls' fabric.

There are two important insights to understanding the grief process:

The stages of grief are fluid. You move in and out, return, pass over, skip, or linger. The order and speed at which each person travels through grief is individualized to his or her own needs.

The most difficult stage to traverse and pass is the yearning stage.

Science may have given order to the bereavement process, but the individuality of each person conforms the process to meet his uniqueness. (For example, you may quickly pass through the anger stage, while your spouse may linger there for months. You may skip a stage, to return to it at a later time in your grieving process. Your spouse may move slowly, but consistently through each stage.)

The yearning stage involves two of Elisabeth Kübler-Ross's steps: anger and depression. When your child dies, the emptiness encompasses you. It seems impossible to continue life with such a void. You feel a physical ache, a deep yearning for the child. Emptiness transfers to a longing that you try to fill with something—a hobby, new job, or new child—anything that you hope will make the pain go away. Nothing stops the emptiness.

Bitterness and anger become bed partners. Resentment toward God, the medical help, family members, friends, self begin to destroy you.

Or you may be able to move into yearning without the bitterness and anger. Still you grieve. For months your mind entirely focuses on your deceased child. No matter how intensely involved in other activities, the backdrop of your thoughts will be your loss. This stage can last months, years, a lifetime. Release comes when you let go of the yearning for life to be what it was before the death.

Grief Is a God-Given Healing Process

So often, as Christians, when we experience this spiral of grief, of separateness, we feel deep guilt. If we were living our faith, we would not experience such anguish. Wouldn't real faith mean trusting God so much that whatever happened would not be questioned? Shouldn't we feel a sense of joy at knowing our child is with God? If we trusted in God's design for life, why would we wallow in the mire of sorrow?

Grief work is God's process. If He had wanted us to instantly be freed from our emotional turmoil, following a death, we would not travel the standard path. A growth transpires in the bereavement, if we allow it. God undergirds and gives a peace that is not understandable until we have experienced it. The emotions are helter-skelter, but underneath, behind the scenes, embedded in the semiconscious is the *knowledge*, not feeling, that God has us in His care.

There are many helps to surviving, but only one key. The key is *acceptance!—not acceptance of your loss, rather acceptance of the grief process*. You must accept the pain and hurt as you accept happiness and love. Grief emotions are part of a God-given process.

You will not accept your child's death until you have completed the healing. Hurt, anguish, tears, yearning, pining are part of the healing. There is no way to turn loose of a child without the accompanying suffering. But with the dragging days, hold to the hope and knowledge that the mind and emotions do heal—if you make the right choices!

Knowing and experiencing are very different encounters.

I knew the stages of grief. I had taught a course on grief. But no one could have explained the shock phenomena to me. Authors write about shock, but there was more to our emotional state than could be defined in such a narrow term. We were overcome by God's presence.

LeeAnne's vital signs of life were fading. The medical machinery had been able to stay death only two days. As the staff removed the medical paraphernalia, we gathered our tiny, precious child's limp body in our arms. In minutes she would be gone—but not without our presence and touch. If her purpose in life were over, she needed us to comfort her as she moved into a new world. It was not shock, but love that gave us the strength to hold her quietly, tears falling.

LeeAnne, don't be afraid. Booma is waiting for you. Heaven is beautiful, LeeAnne. Remember the times we talked about God, the littlest angel—maybe you can be the littlest angel's best friend. You can tell him about your acrobatic tricks and learning to ride a bicycle. Won't it be special for God to show you His wonderful treasures? You are going to be all right, honey. We are holding you. You are going to be safe.

As she breathed her last breath, a tear ran down LeeAnne's cheek.

Then the shock began. Numbness. Slowed movements. Inability to think or focus. From the moment of death until the day after the funeral, life became third-person nonreality. I am here, but not here. When the reality would creep in, the pain that accompanied it brought back the numbness, the slowed movements. God, I know You love LeeAnne and You love us. But are You sure this is right?

Three

The Initiation Into Grief _____

Don't tell anyone whose child is about to die that there are things worse than death, even if it is true. Don't tell anyone that giving up a child for adoption must be worse than giving up a child to death, even if you think that at least with death the pain is ended. Don't tell a parent that, unless after you have gone to the funeral home to choose a casket for your own child, you still feel death is the easier alternative. Still, perhaps you should wait until you see them lower the coffin with your child into the ground.

I wasn't "me" at the funeral home. "Me" was some-
where else. A third person sat with Paul in front of the
funeral director's desk. Details. Clothes. Notifications.
Service times. Someone else heard the director comment, "Sorry. We don't have too many caskets for your
choice. In fact, we only have this one. Children don't die
often. It must have been two or three years ago that we
used the last child's casket."

All I knew as I sat there was we could not leave
LeeAnne at this beautiful funeral home. She wouldn't
like it, and we might not survive the rites.

The Rites Begin

It wasn't that my husband and I had never experienced a
child's funeral before. We had traveled widely and had seen
death in various cultures.

In the rarely visited backland country of Thailand, where
motorized vehicles can only travel three months of the year,
we encountered a Thai tribe in the midst of funeral rites. A
young boy had died. The whole community was in mourning.
Men, adorned in their finest dress, huddled together, building
a wooden casket. The women braided a burial blanket. They
were smoking, sharing stories of their times with the child,
laughing, crying. The villagers were being comforted in the
loss by the knowledge that the boy, though deceased, was
intertwined with their experiences and shared memories.

In Bethlehem we watched as family and friends, dressed in
black, carried a dead child on a sling above their heads. Their
voices joined in a wailing sound that sent mournful shivers over
all those who heard. There was no question that the child's
death meant grief. The funeral procession marched up and
down the narrow, winding streets, announcing the anguish by
their dress and lamenting. All ages joined to uphold one another. The focus was on the loss, however, not on the joy the
life had brought to each person, as in the Thai funeral rites.

A procession in Haiti for a deceased baby was neither

comforting nor mournful. Village children, dressed in their best, carried a small box to the cemetery common hole. The child was placed in the group burial plot. Children threw flowers into the grave. There were no tears, and the children seemed untouched by the death as they smiled and laughed to people on their route. At home the family had continued with their daily routines, barely acknowledging the ache that filled the parents' hearts. The death of a child was a normal occurrence in the village routine. There was no time to deal with rites when daily living demanded every energy.

But never before had it been *our* child!

When your child dies, you need to carefully consider the rules of the last rites. The shock, disbelief, and empathy of the community gives these rites far more impact. Do what you feel will help your family begin to heal.

The rituals surrounding a death are crucial rites of passage. Funeral rites serve seven crucial functions:

1. The rites begin the acceptance of the reality of the death.
2. They are filled with symbols that return to warm and support us when the cold, stark reality seems overbearing.
3. They provide a social support system.
4. Guidelines for mourning are provided.
5. The letting go of the body is made less difficult.
6. The services provide the only place where most people receive firsthand education about death.
7. The services provide a spiritual undergirding and structure for our religious beliefs.[1]

Here's how we handled each stage of the rites. (For additional information, *see* Appendix I.)

The Visitation

Rather than following the convention of funeral-home visitation, we chose to have LeeAnne's visitation in our home.

No, it was not horrendous. We found it less painful than leaving Lee in her casket in the funeral home. We were in a total fog anyway. The knowledge that she was in our home, as opposed to a silent room, alone, in the funeral home was comforting. We knew Lee was safe in God's arms, but psychological "letting go" of the body involves more than knowledge. It is incredibly difficult.

We also chose to close LeeAnne's casket. Our last memories of her were the farewell in the hospital. When her spirit left, LeeAnne was no longer there. We could see that difference. We wanted to remember, and we wanted others to remember, our bubbly, vivacious, charming child.

The imprint upon one's mind of a child in a casket is indelible. It would have been devastating to hear comments about how good LeeAnne looked. She looked *dead*. There is no question in anyone's mind when a child dies as to its reality, regardless of the viewing or not viewing of the body. The death can be read in every face.

The advantages of having the visitation in our home, as opposed to the funeral home, were numerous:

1. *Comforting:* LeeAnne was still home—with her family!
2. *Less formality:* The atmosphere allowed a more at-ease sharing, crying, opening-up time.
3. *Expanded level of emotional support:* Extended family, friends, children could talk, move around to see other friends, linger.
4. *More comfortable:* Home furnishings, tables of food, different seating areas provided more comfort.
5. *Luxury of escape:* Family members needing a reprieve from visitors and sharing could escape to a bedroom, bathroom, a bed, to relax or simply cry alone.
6. *Afforded play areas:* Children could attend, feel comfortable, escape to play areas, visit LeeAnne's room.
7. *Additional focuses:* As opposed to the family being the only focus, as at the funeral home, the home provides scrapbooks, food, pictures, home furnishings that draw

the conversations away from total absorption with the death.

A small home, even an apartment, should not deter home visitation. Being crowded at such times provides comfort. People talk more freely and informally than when the surroundings are quiet and, though lovely, sterile. Problems with parking can be solved by the funeral home or family friends.

Graveside Service

The most difficult part of the ritual services is the interment. For this reason, we changed the order of the services and held the graveside service prior to the funeral service. (The interment was at 10:00 A.M., the service of celebration at 4:00 P.M.)

Joining family and close friends at the gravesite, we had a simple service around the casket. Once we reached the site, we formed several circles around the casket, our bodies touching, our arms around one another.

Gary Smith's voice softly filled the morning air with "Surely, the Presence of the Lord Is in This Place." Our minister then began an open prayer time with a simple prayer of thanksgiving for LeeAnne's little life. Quietly, friends and family lifted their prayers, thanking God for LeeAnne and for His undergirding strength. Simple. Quiet. Touching. We left with a numbing, bottomless sadness. But we were not *annihilated!*

The Funeral Service

For the church service, we requested a service of celebration that would focus on LeeAnne's life. The half hour prior to the celebration service, bright, light, bubbly music was played on the piano. The songs rang with cheer, childish laughter, and love of life. Our sensitive and gracious minister opened and closed the service with uplifting remarks about

LeeAnne, the value of her life, and the hope of eternal life and comfort. In lieu of a sermon, the congregation was invited to share a favorite memory of LeeAnne.

Reverend Ernest Cushman began: "We are here to celebrate a wonderful little life, a life that made everyone happy who knew her, a likeable person who had a way of brightening the day for those who crossed her path." A prayer of thanks for LeeAnne's life was lifted, followed by a trilogy of bright, uplifting songs: "Little Flowers," "Because He Lives," and "Surely the Presence of the Lord Is in This Place." To initiate the sharing, Reverend Cushman said, "All day today I have had the image of a pebble tossed into a pond. A large pebble creates a large circle of ripples. A small pebble creates ripples, too. Even though LeeAnne was a little girl, her life, the ripples she created, intersected our lives in many ways."

I stood first, because she was my child, because I wanted to thank God for her precious life and thank those who had worked so hard to save her from death and those who had touched her life in wonderful ways. I wanted to share the blessing she had been to us. Also, I wanted to encourage others to share their thoughts with us, because when the service was over, we would need their spoken words to encourage us.

Anecdotes volleyed like popcorn throughout the congregation. Children and adults stood to share the way their lives had intersected with LeeAnne's: a teacher, the school crossing guard, a friend, the custodian, a neighbor, a church acquaintance. There was laughter at the thought of Lee peering around the church pew, to see if she was the only one joining the minister for the children's sermon; tears when her choir teacher talked of needing her to set the pitch for the children's choir; smiles when a neighbor reminisced about LeeAnne's pirouetting across their yard, dressed in a ballerina tutu, stopping to climb a tree.

Some comments were more serious. An aunt shared that loving LeeAnne had given her a way to show LeeAnne's parents how much she loved them. A friend commented that watching LeeAnne handle shots and the difficulties of diabetes with a happy smile made her feel she could handle her own problems, too. A teenager remarked he hoped his life could reach out to others, like LeeAnne's.

No one left the service without the distinct impression of the value and intertwining of our lives upon one another, regardless of age. It was beautiful. The service was uplifting.

Another plus for a sharing service is its focus. The loss is such a quicksand—swallowing, engulfing, pulling, and strangling. Dwelling on something positive is a lifeline to sanity in the midst of horror. Our thoughts were drawn to the value of Lee's life. The nights before the service, we lay in a sleepless stupor, focused on sharing the beautiful ways LeeAnne enriched our lives. Gratitude to others for the many ways they had reached out to LeeAnne filled our hearts.

After the service, we benefited from an unexpected spinoff. People who had not commented in the service, wrote: "As I listened to others talk about LeeAnne, I wanted to share the way she has touched my life. . . ." The blessings of the service of celebration continued long after its completion.

Four

If Only
I Had More Faith _____

Lord,

If You let her go, if her purpose here was
over, why did You leave such a void? I'm
so empty. Don't You care? Why haven't you
filled me with peace, acceptance? Why
is there such pain?

Your word is filled with promises. Why don't
You work them in my life? If it is true that I must let

go, why don't You take away the yearning?
How do I turn loose, Lord, how?

Oh God, it hurts! It hurts! I just want
someone to take care of me, someone to take
away the ache. How much longer, Lord,
before there is acceptance?

Please, please take the desire away.

It is sad to lose a child, but even more sad to feel that if you had had more faith, your child would have survived. Tragically you watch as shadows from plunging emotions cast shadows upon your faith. *If only I had trusted more. . . . If I could have prayed more fervently. . . . If my life had been more faithful, maybe He would have heard. . . .*

When Prayer "Doesn't Work"

The Bible is filled with miracles that changed lives, restored health, and overcame all obstacles. When trust joins belief, miraculous intervention comes, moving mountains and altering the inevitable. No question, faith is the ticket to well-being. Then why did our child die when we had faith?

We prayed and prayed and pleaded! Why were our prayers rejected? The faith was there; the petition was there; God's caring was there. If faith is the answer, if prayer offered by multiple believers is the answer, if trust is the answer, something went wrong.

When prayer is rejected, you question your understanding of God. Or if you accept that your child's death was within the will of God, the depth of emotional emptiness tears you asunder. Questions rip through your mind: *Why doesn't God take away this pain? Why can I not handle my grief? If I trust God's love for me, why can't I let go?* Obviously, there is a conflict: In the midst of faith, some prayers work while others fail.

The problem is prayer has three elements: faith, petition, and God's will. Overemphasis on two of the three essentials, asking and faith, creates misunderstanding. We ignore the third element of prayer: God's will. If the prayer succeeds, we credit the miracle to faith and God's answering. If it fails, we question whether there was enough sincerity or trust or wonder if we sinned. We do not consider God's plan may be different from our petition. Such conflict causes confusion.

Christ was in perfect communication with God when He prayed that His life be extended. His emotional plea was replete with such urgency and physical exhaustion that the sweat from his brow was like drops of blood. He embodied the perfect elements: faith, lack of sin, and earnest petition. Nevertheless, He was crucified. God did not grant His prayer. Judging Christ's prayer in human terms, on the basis of faith and petition, it failed. However when we judge that way, we overlook the fact that God's will is the critical factor, because He alone knows the total design of life.

Our view of life is bound by the limits of time. God has no such handicap. His overview is boundless. As if He were over a city in a helicopter, He is able to see what happens everywhere at the same time. Because He watches the progression without the hindrances of buildings, walls, or visual blocks, He knows about events before they materialize.

God's Permissive Will

Did God zap LeeAnne? No, I don't believe He caused her death. But if I believe God is actively involved in my life, I must also believe He permitted her death. He allowed the natural consequences of the disease process, even as He was caring for our family, watching over LeeAnne.

God's permissive will has three conditions:

1. God's ultimate plan will not be defeated.
2. Good can come from the tragedy.
3. God understands and empathizes with our suffering.[1]

When LeeAnne died, we did not question that her death was in the will of God. Though our prayers were zealous,

God's design for LeeAnne's life was different from that of our pleas. The events surrounding LeeAnne's death leave no doubt that God not only knew LeeAnne would die, He protected and sheltered us, her family, from additional grief. Let me share several events that reinforced our knowledge of His care throughout the tragedy.

Though Paul and I had decided to have no more children because of the time demand of LeeAnne's diabetes, I conceived a fourth child. I was distraught by the certain knowledge that this new child was a replacement for my youngest daughter. With Brad's birth and the continued good health of LeeAnne, my intuitive feeling subsided and our family seemed even more complete. Brad was two when we buried LeeAnne. He was not a replacement. He was a gift. His two-year-old age demanded our love, attention, and time. Thank God for Brad.

Being a medical doctor, Paul would have dealt with tremendous guilt if LeeAnne had died at home. The night her violent illness began, Paul and I were out of town, visiting friends with whom we planned to stay the weekend to reminisce about fun times in Europe, common business interests, and of course our children. We were overcome with a sense of urgency to return home.

Arriving home, we found the grandparents anxious about LeeAnne's sudden vomiting and hysterical crying. From that moment, we did not leave LeeAnne's bedside. Though all physical symptoms led Paul and the pediatricians to feel LeeAnne's weakening condition was merely because of flu, a sense of apprehension gripped us.

Sleeping fitfully the second night, Paul suddenly bolted from the bed. As I tucked LeeAnne into a blanket to ward off the cold in the car, Paul called the pediatricians to meet him at the hospital emergency room. Three hours later, after verification by the surrounding doctors that all vital signs were in sync, LeeAnne died in her daddy's arms. It was not chance that compelled Paul to seek help at the hospital at 4:00 A.M. It was God preventing years of misgiving and additional pain for Paul. Thank You, God!

Three months before this tragic morning, my extended family had encircled LeeAnne and Roy Bowie, my father, to pray for their restored health. Dad had cancer, LeeAnne, diabetes. Within two weeks my father lay in intensive care, battling for his life against cancer, Pseudomonas (a bacterial infection), and enterovirus. Within weeks the combination of diseases had weakened this athletic, virile man to the point where he could not speak, recognize anyone, or lift his fingers off his sheets. Death sat on his bed.

Groups throughout the country prayed for my dad. The morning Paul carried LeeAnne into the hospital where she died in his arms, my dad left the same medical center, a declared miracle. Many of the same groups prayed for LeeAnne during the two and half days the machines stayed her inevitable final death. We never questioned the possibility of Roy's recovery, nor did we question that LeeAnne would recover if it were God's will. Our prayers for both were answered, not the way we expected, but filled with drama that showed us God was in control. Roy's mission on this earth was not completed; LeeAnne's was finished. Both were healed.

Though there were major confirmations of God's overseeing protection, many smaller coincidences affirmed the same care. I had not ordered stationery for ten years, but several weeks before LeeAnne's death, while visiting a local printer for another reason, I decided to order personalized notecards. The week LeeAnne died, 400 notecards arrived which we used to write thankyous. Arriving in Knoxville for the reunion celebration unexpectedly early, Paul and I decided to shop for a sports jacket and slacks for our growing teenage son. By these purchases, we were saved from concern over his wardrobe needs five days later at his sister's funeral. A week before Lee's death I spied a wonderful dress in my favorite dress shop, perfect for my teenage daughter's wedding in umpteen years or some special occasion. The occasion was Lee's funeral.

Even though these were trivial matters, shopping in the midst of grief would have been difficult. Having problems as minor as clothes for the family solved left energy for the more important aspects of death.

The Sunday morning before LeeAnne died, she had been completely mesmerized by the sung benediction, "Surely the Presence of the Lord Is in This House." As we sat, Lee stood and sang the song with the choir. We reached to silence her, then stopped. She was emotionally part of the song. That song filled our minds, was central to each of her services, and was a key to filling us with peace. It seemed as if the vivid picture of her singing the song was part of the overall design to comfort our family through such a tragic period.

LeeAnne's body continued to live for almost three days after the doctors hooked her to the medical machinery. As I watched her, held her, talked to her, listened to the hinted "hopelessness," I refused to think that she might die. Responding to a feeling of urgency, a dear friend en route to a meeting, stopped at the hospital to offer to drive to Williamsburg to bring our daughter home from college. I declined the offer. Lee was stable; Kim was taking mid-term exams. Suzie asked me to consider letting Moody Aviation fly to Williamsburg to bring Kim home for the day.

I went home to change clothes. As I entered the door, the phone was ringing. It was Kim, wanting to come home. "Finish the day's exams," I told her. "We will have a Moody plane in Williamsburg for you this afternoon." Kim arrived home, came straight to the hospital, and spent several hours with LeeAnne, sharing her love and tears. Our family was together the next morning, surrounding Lee as she died. Gratitude to God fills my heart whenever I think of His watching over each one of our family.

The morning of Lee's final departure, a friend invited me to breakfast in the hospital cafeteria. As I left the table my final remark to her was "Jo, I know LeeAnne will be totally healed or she will not make it." I had never considered the possibility of Lee's death until that remark. God wouldn't leave her handicapped—blind, brain damaged, unable to walk. I'm grateful the words were in my mind as we faced pulling away the medical apparatuses binding her body to life one hour later.

These and other uncanny circumstances dramatically pointed out that LeeAnne's death was not chance. God was with us; His love was obvious; His concern for even the small details was evident. Though His will was different from ours, our prayers were heard. Lack of faith had nothing to do with her death or our emotional plunge after her death.

Even as we watched Lee's life ebb away, we knew that God held the controls. Faith is a walk based on knowledge that God guides, cares, and has our ultimate good in His design; it is not based on feelings. There was no reason to doubt our faith. But would anything ever heal our spiraling emotions?

Five

Is This Healing? _____

I have got to stay. I can do it! . . . No! No! I can't. I am going to die. My mind is going to die. I am blowing up like a tire, getting tighter, tighter. My body is exploding. God, something is gutting me from the inside. I feel it. It's not my imagination. Something is tearing me apart. Maybe, if I turn up the music a little louder. . . .

All I can do is run. I run in one direction, then another. I hit a wall, a mountain falls on me. My stomach churns, wrenches. Every emotion collides, cascading, rolling, and finally avalanching into the total panic. There are no tears. I am immobilized—except I can't stop moving. If I could just open the door, I could leave. The rooms are throwing bars across the escapes. I have to stop thinking. I have to make it. God, I can't!

This was the most horrible day of my life. The day LeeAnne died was devastating; the day she was buried had been inconceivable, but this day, the day life was supposed to return to normal, was annihilation. I had reached a state of sheer panic. So devastating was the pain inside me that I could not breathe, think, or reason. My hand could not reach the telephone to call a friend. I couldn't scream. I couldn't cry. I had to stay! I had to face a day alone—or the healing could never begin. Please, God, don't let me ever have to do it again. I would rather be dead.

Healing? This sheer terror, confusion, inability to focus a thought, emotional mayhem is healing? It is like living in an ocean, with every function moving in waves—up, down, crashing, peaking, flat.

The designs for healing of the body and mind are elaborate, complex, orderly systems. Though each system works in a predictable, step-by-step progression, the body's healing system has a significant difference from the mind's process. The body works automatically; the mind chooses to accept healing.

Observing the healing of a skin cut illuminates the body's complex programmed pattern. When a cut alerts the chemical emergency system of the body to send macrophages, the macrophage cells form a cleanup detail to surround and carry away the debris of dead cells, clotted blood, and matter from the laceration. They also initiate stimuli that cause new cell growth. Nearby cells release fluid to stimulate the flushing and clotting. As the cells pull the cut tissue together with a scar, a scab forms over the cut. In the final stage the scab falls off, leaving the new scar tissue binding the cut.

The same orderliness takes place as the mind and emotions heal. Before we complete the healing, we must traverse predictable emotional and mental cycles. Yet where the body functions respond automatically, the mind and emotions must choose to initiate the plan for their healing: They can accept no healing, partial healing, or complete healing. Healing is a choice of the mind.

Logic cannot explain the subconscious, God-directed hand that guides you through these choices, if you listen. Behind the emotional turmoil lies a subliminal urging to direct your path out of the catacombs of despair. Using the quiet directives, your befuddled mind must pull fragmented emotions into sync.

Dealing with the emotions, overcoming their control of mind and body, is like walking a tightrope. A delicate balance exists between reason and emotion, and using reason becomes difficult when a watermelon of out-of-control emotions has been put into your apartment-sized mental refrigerator. The watermelon wants to push everything else aside. To remove it, the emotions must be consumed slowly. Trying to eat too quickly will give you stomach cramps. Trying to overlook, hide, and cram normal emotions back into the space around it does not work.

Paul tried valiantly to reenter his working world immediately after LeeAnne's rites. As patients offered condolences, he mouthed clichés to prevent real emotional contact. Without putting up a wall around his hurt, he couldn't function as a physician. Bit by bit the crowded emotions began to seep out, until one afternoon fear gripped him. He could not remember LeeAnne's face. Guilt and panic pushed him to a psychiatrist's counsel. No, he had not forgotten his daughter. He had stuffed his feelings behind words, disallowing his heartache.

In grieving, reason often allows the emotions to take control of our life. The emotions demand suicide, giving up, and hiding. When issues outside yourself seem trite, insignificant, and piddling, feeling good is tough. It is hard to pull your emotions into line to participate in normal activities with friends and family.

My reentry was a friend's baby shower. I found it unbelievably tough to make myself get out of the car, enter the home, and act normal. Nothing about me felt normal. I could not laugh or even smile and felt isolated, different, outside. These friends could have been total strangers. We walked on different planes. The group understood; they were not expecting me to feel like "Betty."

The body heals automatically; the mind and emotions heal by choice.

A stream of thinking patterns evoked by grief causes feelings of isolation. Knowing these feelings are normal allows your reasoning power to remain calm and work through the accompanying emotional drain. Controlling the emotions takes time. Reason can win, but not without a struggle.

Emotion-Controlled Thinking Patterns

Five patterns of thought, controlled by the emotions, vie for command of our actions. Either we rein in the emotions or they run away, creating havoc in every area of our lives.

I'm Going Crazy

Wouldn't this thought enter your mind, if you could no longer think coherently, with thoughts flashing in and out, emotions up and down, your ability to remember completely obliterated? After the death of your child, your mind seems detached from your body. Your vocabulary is jumbled. This lasts for weeks, maybe months.

I'm Different

Feeling isolated is lonely, but normal. You are different— along with millions of others. The tragedy has happened to you. With it comes the reality, either accepting your difference as normal or spending your life pining.

If you choose to accept your child's death as a handicap, you feel you have a legitimate right to be pitied. Losing a child is the ultimate grief. There is luxury in feeling one is a victim of life, because it brings attention and offers an excuse to shrug off life's responsibilities. Expressing and sustaining resentment and anger are easier than accepting the loss. The problem is you can't be happy with a "victim attitude." It destroys you, your family, and friendships.

I'm Hallucinating

Studies show almost one-fifth of those who experience a child's death will have a direct sensory experience.[1] Debates wage between the "wishful thinking" opponents of hallucinations and the "firsthand experience" proponents. Parapsychologists indicate these experiences reveal a realm of consciousness that is slowly being uncovered through research. Psychologists feel the bereaved is reaching out for evidence that his loved one continues to live.

Paul and two-year-old Brad were in our swimming pool when they heard the sounds of someone jumping on the trampoline in the exercise room. Brad wanted to play with the acrobat, as he had with LeeAnne. Paul, knowing there could be no person in the room, joined Brad with intention of shooing away the dog that must have entered the trampoline room through a back door. To their surprise the room was empty. Paul was filled with a sense of LeeAnne's presence, as was Brad, who immediately wanted to know where LeeAnne had gone.

Paul's inner reaction was a sense of peace. When he related the experience to me, I responded with distress. We had been doing a pretty good job of loving our little girl. If heaven were so much better and joyful than earth, why would LeeAnne return spiritually? I wondered. Maybe she felt lonely. Nevertheless, Paul was confident about the experience's reality. It was difficult to confront our two-year-old's simultaneous encounter.

If you experience hallucinations after your child's death, do not be alarmed. However, if the hallucinations continue for an extended period of time—or are threatening—seek professional help. You are not crazy, but may need to work through problems with your acceptance of the death. Counselors are aware of the conflicting debates on direct sensory encounters and will be sensitive to your experience. They can offer third-person evaluation.

I Can't Stand This Pain

The numbing quality of shock momentarily keeps reality at bay. Then the impact hits with full force. *Torment, affliction, agony, suffering, misery, nightmare, distress, heartache, sorrow, woe:* No word seems adequate. The mind, emotions, and body are disrupted by the vortex of spinning miseries. Confronting the anguish takes courage.

The approval given to drugs is the greatest tragedy allowed bereaved parents. As Elisabeth Kübler-Ross said, "It's criminal! It's criminal to give drugs to dull the grief process."[2] I was offered drugs from the moment I learned of LeeAnne's plight, but how grateful I am I did not take them. Drugs postpone, but do not stop the inevitable anguish. By the time most bereaved begin to pull away from this numbing crutch, the support system of friends and family has withdrawn. They face the stunning reality of their child's death without the bolstering props of understanding friends and family.

I'm So Sorry

I'm sorry for everything I did not do right, everything I should have done, everything I wish I had thought to do—for my child, for my entire life.

Guilt comes packaged with death. Sigmund Freud described their interaction when he said, "All relationships are characterized by ambivalence, feelings of both love and hate."[3] So the loss of a loved one creates an unconscious sense of guilt. Dealing with guilt in your relationship with the deceased child is part of grieving. The guilt spreads from the deceased to the entire life failures of the bereaved. Introspection that comes with death offers the opportunity for new insights into the meaning of life.

LeeAnne had a physical problem that had demanded our constant attention and love. Therefore we gave her 100 percent of ourselves, loving her unconditionally. She was a blessing to our whole family, and never a day passed that we did not thank God for her. As a result, we did not experience guilt for "lack" of doing the right things for her. We had done our very best to make Lee's life special, and she had returned that love to us, filling our lives with a special joy.

Though I felt positive about my dealing with LeeAnne, evaluation of my life and guilt filled my mind. The good and bad of life flashed, lingered, stayed with me, demanding my attention. It was not painful, just sorrowful. In a flash of reality, I realized the fragility of life. Life is too short to waste time on negative lingering thoughts, misgivings; it is too special to waste energy. Every personality is unique—to be loved. The evaluation allowed a "forgiving" spirit—forgiving others, yes. But mainly forgiving myself. This is God's gift in grief.

In addition to this type of evaluation, Paul dealt with the guilt of not preventing LeeAnne's death. Nothing had been overlooked; she received the best care today's medicine can offer. *If only I could have done something—anything—she wouldn't have died* rang continuously in his thoughts. His reaction was normal; he wanted his little girl.

I Can't

I can't go. I can't call anyone. I don't want to do anything. Insecurity walks hand-in-hand with inability to make decisions after your child's death. The will to do anything is weak.

To decide something, initiate it, do it requires effort. It isn't that you wouldn't if you could. If someone would tell you to do it, you would. There is too much confusion. In addition, you know there is no wall of protection around you—no laughter, quick wit, or lighthearted conversation.

For healing to take place, you must venture away from your protected harbors. The *I can't*s want to hold you, bind you, keep you from moving out or accepting help. Your knowledge that healing will take place as you allow yourself to reenter life can give you the strength to say "I can!" Your focus must move from self to others.

In his ministry, Dr. Bill Gillham tells a story of an Alaskan pioneer who was terrified of a giant polar bear. The polar bear had eaten his partner, snowboots and cap included. While away from his cabin, the pioneer sensed he was being watched. Sheer terror gripped him as he turned to see the dreaded bear, arms raised, mouth open. The pioneer didn't wait to ask the bear's intentions, nor did he pause to consider if the bear might look good in a zoo. He fled.

Fortunately, he saw a deserted miner's cabin. Making it to the cabin in the nick of time, he slammed the door, barring it with a beam made from a five-foot-wide timber. The bear was thwarted. However, the pioneer did not feel relieved. He felt horrendous fear. As he began to calm, his emotions would pitch to frantic heights each time the monstrous polar bear growled or knocked his body against the cabin door. Though his reason knew the polar bear could not get into the cabin, his emotions took hours to settle, cresting, flattening, peaking, and calming.[4]

Like the pioneer, you begin to control your emotions step by step. You realize one day seems less painful. A ray of joy, a moment of release from the bondage of your yearning thoughts shines through the depression. Perhaps, two or three days will pass with no major emotional collapse. Then the emotions escalate, and again you are in the throes of depression. The cycle will repeat, but the time between plunges will grow longer.

Following the instructions of your reasoning, when your emotions are pitching and screaming, is like remaining calm when the ship is sinking: It's hard. Yet you *can* allow your reason to have control. Allowing reason, instead of the emotions, to lead is a matter of choice.

Six

Hurting on the Inside _____

After the death of your child, escapes seek you. You must *choose* coping techniques.

Nighttime is a threat. I lie in bed, awaiting blessed sleep, exhausted, wanting "out" for a few hours. Nothing. My body is fatigued from "acting normal" during the day, but my mind cavorts with memories. The quiet allows it to play, running helter-skelter, pell-mell into thoughts of LeeAnne. Senseless to lie here, waiting for my body to join my thoughts, waiting for it to move from simple streams of tears, to sobs, to washing heaves.

I take a mundane, nonaddicting drug that helps bring sleep—*aspirin*. Aspirin slows the mental activity, allowing the mind to follow the body to sleep. But sometimes—like tonight—it doesn't succeed. Why should I allow my body to be filled with the ache that begins in the middle and spreads to every point, crying out for LeeAnne's touch? Quietly, I roll out of bed to avoid awakening Paul—who lies sleepless, too.

I turn on the VCR. For someone who rarely watched television, I have changed dramatically. I now avidly consume movies in the wee hours of morning. I watch until my mind begs my body to sleep. Or I write. I write my hurt. On the typewriter, I beg God to give us peace. I write every thought. Then I rewrite until the focus becomes the quality of writing, not the memories. I write until my eyes begin to shut and my mind slows.

I was offered drugs to dull the pain—the pain of those watching me grieve and my own pain. Everyone wanted to help me cope. I would have paid almost anything to have the hurt disappear, but the cost of drugs was too high.

The coping drugs, tranquilizers like Librium and Valium, slow the body and mind activities. You walk through activities as an outsider whose sidekicks are nagging, nudging undercurrents of distress. The body is garbed as a knight in tranquility, ready to cope. But the knight has no confrontations. Then, when he has put aside the drugs, the knight must fight a nudging that has exploded into full, agonizing reality. Without his armor of drugged protection, he has been allowed no slowed increments of acceptance, as in normal grief. His support groups are gone, his family is in disarray, his child is still dead, and he is expected to be far down the road of recovery. Too costly for me. I am a coward at facing pain alone.

My eyes hurt. I could model for "before" pictures for eye drops to get the red out. Over-the-counter drugs for

red, swollen eyes do nothing, except add to the pool of
moisture in my eyes. An ophthalmologist suggests several eye drops that constrict the blood vessels and reduce
inflammation, available with prescription. They feel so
good. Aching eyes are unnecessary. My energy needs to
go to other demands.

Healing for Hurts

How long is this grieving supposed to last? A friend told me
she could remember standing at her kitchen window, two
years after her child died, tears streaming. Two years is
eternity. Every time I begin to feel a day or two of release, I
am thrust into the whirlpool again. As the days move to
weeks, I begin to feel hope that life will continue. Then a
holiday comes. I try to not think about the time being special.
I add activities—a party for the children, dinner for friends, or
shopping. But as the "special" day creeps closer, an empty
swelling begins to consume my insides. It arrives, and I am a
shell with a "Betty" for the outside.

I don't even remember the exact day LeeAnne died. I have
to think hard to pull it to the surface. This happened Sunday,
so this happened Monday, so she died on Tuesday—or was it
Wednesday? I won't focus on that. I will focus on her
birthday—after all it was only a week away. That is a happier
thought. Would I give a talk on LeeAnne's death day? Sure.
I need to stay extra busy that day, anyway.

As her death day approached Paul and I did not talk about
LeeAnne's death. We responded internally. Our eyes couldn't
hold the tears again. Thinking was difficult, ideas flighty. A
weight inside our bodies pulled, making it difficult to act
spontaneously. Food lost all taste. Paul and I clung together,
wordless, in need of a touch. The days became increasingly
more difficult.

Then, D day arrived. God, it is almost as bad as the day she
died. I promised to give a talk tonight. Talk? My mind is
defunct. Maybe "Betty" can talk; I am going to die. Betty

will have to play with Brad, pick up Paul Edward at school. She will have to say "hello" to everyone. *She* is going to have to make her mind work—not me. I am going to grieve. I want to wallow in my sorrow. I still want my little girl.

Betty went to the meeting. I came along. How funny to be two people at one time! I could just observe, except "our" psychosomatic stomach grabbed both of us. It wanted to consume us. Betty tried to speak, and the words came out. She tried to focus, and her mind kept a train of thought. Thank You, God. We couldn't have made it without You there. God, thank You for the speech. "I" might have won, if we hadn't had a focus for the day. If "I" had won, Betty and I both would have lost.

I have to face it. Life is never going to be the same again. I can moan, and cry, and be sad, but it won't help the fact that LeeAnne is gone. It is time to stop the grieving. Grieving must change to acceptance, not acceptance of LeeAnne's absence, but acceptance of the fact that I am always going to miss her. I'm not sure you ever really accept the hole in your soul. Instead you decide to continue living with it. You decide to focus on how extra blessed you were without the hole and how blessed you are to be able to enjoy all the abundant blessings around you, even with the hole. So anniversaries will always be hard. Special events or people or places or activities will always jog the memories back to the missing part of your life—and that will always hurt. Yet it will not be as depressing, because you have accepted that hurt is an acceptable emotion.

We are doing something right, Lord. Our friends have not quit talking to us about LeeAnne. That means we have kept the doors open. We have shared our feelings, letting them know how grateful we were that they were willing to be part of our sharing. When they have called to offer help, we have accepted it. We have also reached out to them, letting them know we needed their help.

Don't you know how terrible it is? Wanting to help, but not knowing what to do, afraid to say the wrong thing. So many bereaved say they have no one in whom to confide their grief, no one who cares. It has to be that those who care have been afraid to come. They have felt the closed doors. It's so hard to tell the truth, to say, "I hurt." "No, I'm not doing well. I'm having a hard time." "Can you come over? I need to talk." It's hard, but it has to be easier than trying to stand up alone.

Many people felt embarrassed to mention LeeAnne's name, for fear it would cause us pain. We have tried to overcome this fear by being natural. Where it is not forced, we share comments about LeeAnne, but we have not let our conversations be dominated by remembrances of her. That frees friends and family to follow suit.

I wondered why so many people kept telling me time would help, especially when the days became more devastating as the full reality of her death hit. But they were correct: Time and choice work together to bring healing. Healing does not occur overnight. Like any wound, time dulls the sharpness of the initial stabbing pain. It may tingle, may ache as the years pass, but not with the same intensity of the first weeks and months.

It takes so much effort to disassociate your child from other children of the same age. I love watching LeeAnne's friends grow up. They are not LeeAnne. They are unique, different individuals, and as long as I think of them as who they are, I am fine. The minute I allow questions like *I wonder if LeeAnne would be this tall? Would she like dancing like this now?* to become part of my thinking, the child's uniqueness is lost in generalizations that bring back memories of LeeAnne. Keeping the focus on the child—as opposed to pulling it back to LeeAnne—is hard but worth the effort. LeeAnne gave us the gift of many other friends her age to love through the years; we have a special bond to them through her.

Each of us has different methods of dealing with the pain. Paul revived when he visited the cemetery, but each time I went, I found it debilitating. For me it is hard to focus on my knowledge that LeeAnne is a living spirit, a part of God's continuing plan, when I am centered on her burial plot. Paul sees the plot as symbolic of Lee. There needs to be a middle ground between every-day visitation to the cemetery and never being able to visit. Both extremes can annihilate the family members. Both bespeak denial.

The body was the dwelling place for your child's spirit. Refusing to allow yourself to deal with the body's death is trying to block out the painful remembrances of its loss. On the other hand, constantly dwelling on the habitat of the body overstresses the importance of the physical. Both can be emotional boxes.

Friends and family only have so much patience for grief. We had to begin standing on our own from day one, minute one. Our friends and extended family were supports to lean on—to pull us from the mire of emotional quicksand—but they expected us to make the choices necessary for recovery.

What Does It Take to Survive?

Survival techniques differ as greatly as those who grieve. Some bereaved seek comfort in spending binges: A new trinket, new mechanical apparatus, new car, new dress, any new item offers temporary reprieve from the depression. As long as it does not wreak havoc with your budget, what does it matter? Exercise is great as a tension reliever. Running, walking, swimming, lifting weights, sports offer a way to spin off the punch from bereaved emotions.

Eating your way to obesity, fleeing into overwork, hiding in activity, or burying yourself inside are not good. Ways to escape dealing with your emotions are as numerous as ways to cope. The difference is that *the escapes seek you. Coping techniques, you must choose.* Escapes plead with your emotions and end up creating walls that you must tear down before emotional stability can return.

Take a Break

One of the best survival techniques we used was a trip. As a happy-sixteenth-birthday celebration for Paul Edward, we had scheduled a week-long cruise, to begin two weeks after LeeAnne was admitted to the hospital. So we canceled it, knowing when LeeAnne left the hospital, she would be too weak to handle travel. When she died, we called and rescheduled.

No, we were not callous, nor were we trying to run away. We were not seeking fun and games. Instead we desperately needed to pull our family together—out of college, school, work, and the house. We needed to be away from the memories that draped every activity and place. The minutes that ticked in each hour since her death seemed like eternity. Anguish seemed to have no end.

The trip afforded us a togetherness time—without all the pulls of our individual activities—and thrust us in with people who did not know we were dying inside. Talking to others about something other than our child's absence allowed us to see that the world was continuing to spin. It gave us hope that life could continue for our family unit. So what if we occasionally had tears? Who knew us?

Expect Body Changes

Expect to get sick after tragedy. It isn't psychosomatic. It is a physical response to a crisis of the emotions. The body and emotions work together. When the emotions shout, "Panic," adrenaline pumps. When it shouts, "Tragedy. Sorrow," T-cell production stops. T-cells are integral to the immune system, so the body's protective fighting system weakens. Diseases, viruses, bacterial infections that would normally be too weak to succeed against your defenses attack—and win. Being sick is not in your head, but in your body.

Know also that though you will lose weight at first, you will gain it again within a few months. Watch the scales rise after a day of intense grieving—sans food. Water retention, metabolic slowing, slowed exercise, emotions causing survival techniques within the body—who knows what triggers the phenomenon? There is no need for panic. Your metabolic balance will eventually resettle as the emotional mayhem calms.

Closing the Gap

I have never entertained thoughts of suicide. Even in grief, I did not play with such fantasies. For some, the thought hangs like a noose, beckoning (particularly for teenagers and young adults who have coped with fewer ups and downs in life). If suicide does grip your thoughts, seek counseling help. You may need an outsider to lend help with coping techniques.

We have considered adoption, because the gap left by LeeAnne is too big. Our family seems incomplete. If we could have had another child, we would have! At first, you want a child because you want a replacement, someone who can stop the yearning for the deceased child. If that is your reason, run from the option.

If you have waited through the yearning period and still want another child, because you desire to complete your family with another life to love, consider it strongly. You need to fill that hole. But fill it with a million other options before considering a child. It is unfair to the child who wants your love to feel he is a replacement. Trying to find your deceased child in someone else is unfair to you. Every difference becomes a mountain, every similarity a painful comparison.

The pain inside still hurts. It awakens with me, keeps me company during the day's activities, and joins me in sleep at night. I have chosen to tolerate and accept the pain, because I want to remember LeeAnne. She was a special part of my life. Remembering keeps the hurt alive. But choosing to forget in order to escape the pain is too great a loss.

Seven

Feuding Partners _____

- Three months after our son died, my husband asked for a divorce. First, I lose my son; next, my husband walks out.
- My wife has become a raving lunatic. She talks non-stop: babbles, cries, and screams. There is no peace at home.
- My husband thinks sex will cure the pain. It makes me want to throw up when he touches me.

- She keeps talking about our child all the time. We never go anywhere or do anything that she isn't saying, "Do you remember?" I need to get away from all the memories.
- I know he is seeing someone else. He doesn't come home until late. He doesn't eat here. We can't talk. He doesn't want me to even mention our daughter's name.
- We spend our time together yelling at each other, and what we say hurts. "Letting it all out" is driving us apart.
- My husband blames me for our child's death. He never talks but I feel his accusing stare following me everywhere.
- All he does anymore is talk to the police and cruise the area our daughter was killed. He spends hours on the phone searching for clues, but he won't even talk to me about our other children's needs.
- If only my husband had treated our son better, he wouldn't have killed himself. Now he wants us to act as if our son had never lived. He's my son, too, and I won't put away the pictures or stop mentioning his name!

Who told you tragedy bound husbands and wives together?

It isn't true! Ninety percent of all couples who have lost a child to death have serious marital problems within months of the death of their child. Three out of four divorce within two years.[1]

Why? Because deep pain tends to wrap its victim in a cocoon: You withdraw into yourself; you wander through your activities with *why* echoing in your mind; you are centered on your agony.

Instinctively Paul and I knew the danger ahead for our relationship—for the survival of our family. I could not have survived without him. We clung together, ached together, cried together. We grew closer. We were unusual.

Our survival together was a calculated tactic. The dangers that append to death we had to fight. Failure to confront and overthrow each one leaves a marriage in shambles.

Dangers Ahead

Danger 1: "Do It My Way!"

The first danger to marriage is a belief that states, "My way of grieving is *the way!*" As we became aware of them Paul and I accepted the very different ways each of us expressed our grief. Becoming aware took time.

Watching videos of LeeAnne was Paul's release from his aching loneliness. He and our son would immerse themselves in the movies of LeeAnne skiing, horseback riding, or holding our new baby. They encouraged me to watch, but I could not. Thinking it would be healing for me, several weeks after LeeAnne's death, Paul started a video on the bedroom television. Slipping into bed, I immediately became mesmerized by LeeAnne roller skating, holding the dog, hugging me. My soul ached for her, and I longed to hear her enthusiastic laughter and the words, "Watch me!"

Lee's realness filled my numbed mind, making her absence excruciating. Washing, convulsive heaves threw my body into spasms. I spent the long night hours caught in the vise of unbearable yearning. Videos were a comforting, presence-filling catharsis for Paul, but they destroyed me. Breaking through my protective insulation, they let me feel the full, thrusting hurt of her absence.

My catharsis was reaching out to LeeAnne's friends: Having them visit, taking them places, allowing them to be a continued part of our lives gave me a sense of sharing LeeAnne's love. These were her friends, a part of her. To lose their friendship would be additional grief. Yet Paul felt devastated by their presence—and guilty that he could not handle it. He cared for them, too, but watching them made him miss LeeAnne even more.

Our daughter Kim felt the same need for Lee's friends, plus, we knew the children needed contact with us to handle their own grief. Having a young married adults Sunday-school class campover at our home was the perfect opportunity to have a group of Lee's friends together. They could come for the night, swim, jump on the trampoline, run through the woods, play in LeeAnne's playhouse, and see that life continued for our family.

Kim camped with three of LeeAnne's friends in our backyard, and the next morning the girls prepared an acrobatic show for us. Lee's friends had not been our total focus during the campover, and watching their special presentation tuned in on them, without LeeAnne, who had lived for tumbling and dancing. It was arduous for all of us, but it was unbearable for Paul! He contained his anguish until the girls were gone, but then his unvoiced suffering exploded, shattering the defensive shield around his emotions. The wanting, the hurting, the ache permeated every fiber of his being.

Neither of us tried to "help" the other again by sharing our form of grieving. We realized a critical truth about grief: Everyone is different. In particular, men and women grieve differently. Whether this is due to cultural indoctrination or innate God-designed differences is irrelevant. Marriage partners must appreciate and accept it, because a marriage cannot survive wedges during tragedy. All energy goes to coping with the calamity, and there is none left to mend marital problems.

Men tend to be far less open than women in expressing their emotions. Often they escape from their feelings by deeper commitment to work or hobbies. Women are more enveloped by the emotions, needing to express and talk through how they feel. A wife may think her husband is noncaring and insensitive to his child's death, because he is not outwardly expressive, does not cry, seems reinvolved in his work world. Likewise, a husband may interpret his wife's emotional outpouring, inability to handle social situations, and lack of desire to participate as childish behavior. He may resent her clinging.

Surviving together against this danger demands you become third person to each other. Listen to the hurts, accept the form of grieving as an outsider. Attempting to interject your grief timetable or form upon your partner will build a box around him or her. The box will keep your spouse prisoner—and make you an outsider, unable to share your common tragedy.

Danger 2: "Be Strong"

Another danger that separates a husband and wife is the desire to help the other "be strong." Parts of the death necessities can devastate you or your partner. Each should shoulder the responsibility for needs he or she can handle emotionally.

I found it impossible to deal with two final needs for LeeAnne. Choosing a monument—a grave marker—and having a portrait done from a collage of pictures. Perhaps these would not bother you at all. But even the consideration of the many choices that went into the selection would send waves of grief throughout my body. Both monument and portrait signified "the end" to me. When those selections were over, LeeAnne was gone.

Paul, knowing I literally fell apart trying to deal with the two selections, took over the responsibility. He continued to involve me by asking my preference or showing me designs—enough to grant me the feeling of having a part. Sometimes I could look and listen. Other times the choices would send me on a debilitating spiral.

My love for Paul grew a thousandfold, because he so graciously handled these needs. They both were essentials to completing the memorial for LeeAnne. I desperately wanted the portrait to be wonderful. After all, it was the last portrait of LeeAnne we would give our family, grandparents, aunts and uncles, and cousins. The marker would either comfort us or remind us it was "not right" whenever we visited LeeAnne's memorial.

In this process there were two essential elements to my not feeling guilt bound by inability to "be strong":

> *Small increments of involvement.* Though I told Paul he could
> handle the choices, I wanted to feel part of the process. He

involved me through questions about my desires or opinions. I could look momentarily at the choices, as through a keyhole. If I opened the door fully, the phantoms of hurt grabbed me, flinging me to the floor.

Removal of the guilt. Paul never said, "You need to help me with this. She was your daughter, too." I felt guilty that I could not cope with these needs. A mother should be able to handle the needs of her child—even after death. Today, two years later, thinking about making those choices still brings streams of tears and a bottomless feeling to my stomach.

Danger 3: Change

Death brings change, and change is always tough. Values, priorities, and commitments fall under attack. Like a noose, free time hangs around your neck. Many commitments that hinged on the child have come to a screeching halt. Ways of doing things are altered; nothing seems stable; the simplest of life's daily chores can become poignant, memory-filled challenges. A trip to the grocery store can leave you shattered. Favorite foods, chasing the child through the aisles, stopping-to-get-his-snack-at-the-deli thoughts reduce you to tears.

I remember being "caught" by a child who looked like LeeAnne. She was running up and down the aisles, finding special goodies for her mom, laughing, being enthusiastic and full of life. That little girl was a magnet. My eyes followed her, and my mind ricocheted from one thought of LeeAnne to another. By the time I proceeded to the checkout lane, I felt as if only jumping out a ten-story window would stop the images. If a trip to the grocery store would start the debilitating emotional plunge, how was life ever going to be normal again?

Change pulls away the lifeboat, and you are forced to keep your head above water by endless treading motions. If your spouse levels criticism at the way you are staying afloat, you and your marriage sink. Home needs to be a safe harbor. Unless you plan ways to support each other through this time of reevaluation and alteration, marriage often becomes change's victim.

Danger 4: Make "Me" Happy

Most marriage partners hold the false belief that someone else can make your life happy. If you have not lost a child, you may find it difficult to understand the grieving parent's depth of sadness. You will understand, however, the conflicts caused in marriage because of the integral belief that your partner is supposed to make you happy.

For the first few months, neither partner thinks about happiness. Survival—making it through the day—is all that counts. Then time begins to make grieving seem forever, and the soul becomes weary of being sad. Yet feeling happy when your child is dead makes you feel guilty. "I married you so that you could make me happy!" resentments begin to echo.

Everyone feels uncomfortable with his or her actions, responses, or poignant feelings. Most husbands and wives subconsciously blame these continuing negative emotions on each other. Feuding begins with blame, resentment, and vented hostility. Anger builds because a partner has shirked his or her responsibility to bring happiness.

Recognize this normal pattern. Pull back and evaluate your thoughts. Happiness takes time and many choices. Healing is an arduous process. Be a support and harbor, not the storm. The already endangered marriage will sink with too many high winds.

Paul and I fought these negative seed thoughts. He could not reach out to make me happy when he was devastated. How could I bring lighthearted fun to him when I felt like a rock?

Six months after LeeAnne's death, Paul's gift of a quiet, birthday dinner for two at a local Mexican restaurant was a typical scenario of "fun and celebration" after your child's death. As we carried on a light conversation over tamales, tears began to well, spilling over into the hot sauces. We continued talking as if tears were a normal part of conversation. To celebrate when we felt like dying—and that is the inner sense when your child dies—made no sense. But life had to continue, and we were trying to survive together. We held hands and let the tears flow as we talked about work, friends, chores, and our children. Guilt for celebrating, reality of the unwanted change in life, and remembrances of past birthdays with LeeAnne all meshed in the back of our minds. We tried to laugh, talk, act normal while feeling estranged, different, and miserably unhappy. No telling what the waitress thought!

Some guidelines can prevent tragic miscommunication:

1. Be open to a deeper communication level.
   a. Reach below the surface.
   b. Express your feelings. (There is no energy to guess your partner's underlying emotions.)
   c. Do not use silence. (Your partner will interpret it as a negative response.)
2. Accept responsibility for your own happiness.
3. Be third person in your responses to your partner's unhappy emotions, so that you can work together without being destroyed by each other's grief.

Danger 5: Failing to Meet Your Partner's Ego Needs

Key to marital survival is the meeting of the basic ego needs for both husband and wife.

Everyone, male or female, needs love, but men and women interpret love very differently. Men feel loved when they know they are respected and their sexual needs are met. Women feel loved through tenderness and understanding. These expressions of love fulfill the basic human ego needs.

After tragedy, a woman craves extra outward expressions of tenderness and understanding from her husband; she wants to feel his protective care. Emotions are an endless mire of longing for the child. Touching, holding, cuddling are critical, but she has little or no desire for a full sexual encounter. Who could feel like making love when her child is dead?

Men could! To a man sex says, *I love you. I need you. I care about you.* He relates first sexually, then opens up to verbal communication. Sexual intimacy succors and nurtures the male emotional needs and communicates that he is not standing alone, trying to be strong to support his family and the world's images of himself. Sex allows him to cling, too.

If either husband or wife fails to meet the ego needs, walls will form. Both partners are fragile, insecure, and vulnerable. Meeting your partner's need for love can bind you closely together. Knowing someone loves you, above the tragedies of life, is a security blanket to treasure.

You *must* reach out to each other, because if you fail, your marriage is doomed. If it does survive on those terms, each partner will travel a separate path, having lost the opportunity to become cherished friends, lovers, and teammates.

Danger 6: Surviving Alone

Many survival options after tragedy could be fun alone, running on a single track. A wife could become involved in her social circles. A husband could bury himself in his occupation. Both could absorb themselves in a new hobby or sport, alone. Beware! The threat of isolation is part of the parcel of grief. Togetherness has to be built.

One potentially dangerous survival technique is trying to assuage your grief through consumer products. The need for fulfillment, for something to fill the emptiness, drives you to spending binges. Buying a compact-disc player, a dress, a car, a tennis racket can allow the mind to revel in new thoughts— at least temporarily. No problem, as long as money's not a worry. However, if spending adds to the stress and strife within the home, divert the shopping energy into a new hobby or common interest.

Paul had dreamed of owning Tennessee walking horses. After LeeAnne's death, we decided to develop his dream.

Working and learning together, we went to breeders, horse farms, stockyard sales. Horses were a new world, fun and time consuming. We rode on mountain trails, open pasture, and groomed courses. Horses were a survival technique that I have grown to love doing with Paul; they have become a building block for our togetherness.

The marriage that survives the death of a child includes two people who have calculated their survival. Reasoning, blueprinting a master plan, and analysis are part of the strategies that lead a couple through the maze of downhill emotions. In order for your marriage to survive, it has to become your number-one priority.

But that doesn't mean you can completely forget number two: the children who still survive.

Eight

Children:
The Forgotten Grievers _____

Be sad. Cry. You are looking at the greatest spin-off tragedy emanating from a child's death—destruction of the living children.

Children are often thought to be too young to realize the significance of death. Many of us believe they remain untouched by its meaning. How wrong! Not only does death touch the children, they become its secondary victims. After a sister, brother, or friend's death, they die emotionally or are left crippled, maimed, and handicapped for life.

Few people recognize that children need help to cope with their grief. Children do not understand their own reactions and emotions, so they "act out," and "acting out" brings trouble. Because the parents are so tied in their own grief, they fail to reach out to their living child. That child feels "different." The only way he can break through his parents' deadened emotional response is to strike back. Then the accusations and the comparisons begin, and he loses, because a living child can never be as wonderful as the dead child.

Why do children "act out"? Because the world around them is crumbling. Because they misinterpret their parents' anger and hostility as something they have caused. Because they bear the brunt of much of the anger. Because there is no God—or if there is, who wants Him anyhow?—He took away their sister or brother. He's letting Mom and Dad divorce. He's making the living sister or brother mean. And He doesn't care that there are only tears in this house—and yelling—and nothing. Because the children are forgotten grievers.

Weep for the child who loses a sister. He may never again hear his parents' "I love you." He may never be hugged or kissed. Though he hasn't failed, his parents are so distraught, so angry at God, so afraid to be hurt again that they pull emotional bonding from their remaining child.

Can you hear the little girl's anger? She lost a brother. Her parents have no emotions left, except hurt and bitterness. Caught in their cross fire, she wishes the death had been her own. Then maybe she would be missed, too. Perhaps if she yells, someone will hear her. Maybe if she quits trying, someone will want to make her try again. At least she might get some reaction.

It doesn't have to be like that for the children.

The family can grow closer.
The children can learn to trust God's leading.
They can see their parents overcome a deep loss.
They can know they are loved and treasured.

They can realize the gift of time and life.
They can feel life has purpose.
They can be survivors.

But only if adults help! Too young to overcome the problems of death alone, children either begin to grow with adult help or begin to wither without it. Victoriously dealing with death's hurdles depends upon Mom and Dad's support or another caring adult as a grandparent or family friend.

If you want your children to overcome this challenge, take notice of your living children. You must study their reactions and put every energy into helping them cope. Understand their emotional and reasoning level. Become involved in their lives in a positive way. If you choose to wrap yourselves in your own misery, your living children will become living tragedies—and you won't be able to reverse the damage!

Modern Americans have handled the subject of death with children in the same taboo fashion as sex and money:

Don't talk about it unless the child brings it up.
Don't say too much. (It may be more than the child needs to know.)

Yet nothing in the life of your child will affect him more deeply than the death of his brother, sister, or friend. We think that if children do not bring up the subject, they must be coping well—or have forgotten about the death. We think silence—or a few euphemisms about heaven—will satisfy a child's hurt and curiosity. In our efforts to protect them, we wait for them to ask the questions—*and we are wrong!*

John Bowlby's ground-breaking work on childhood mourning shed new light on the issues of attachment, separation, and loss. In his work *Loss*, Bowlby establishes that children grieve as painfully as adults.

They experience:

1. Fears for personal survival.
2. Separation anxiety.

3. Impaired ability to make emotional attachments.
4. Sadness.
5. Anger.
6. Guilt.
7. Shame.
8. Despair.
9. Problems with control issues.
10. Drops in energy.
11. Loss of self-esteem.
12. Pessimism.
13. Feelings of futility.[1]

Prior to this momentous study, the adult world had considered a child's experience with death to be fleeting. To the adult, the fact that the child usually reentered his world of play or activities meant that he had overcome his brief encounter with bereavement. Bowlby's studies prove that this is not true: A child must move through the stages and responses to grief in a similar pattern to an adult's progression. However, the timing is different, the responses are different, the understanding is different.

Why does a child grieve so intensely? Because believing death can happen to anyone his age is not normal, not a part of his thinking. Death only happens in movies or to old people. When it happens to someone so young, it blows his perception of reality to shattered fragments and makes him feel vulnerable, maybe even guilty. His relationship to the deceased may have been distant—a classmate, a teammate, a student in the same dance program—yet he will tend to idealize the friendship, thinking of the deceased as a dear friend. Children of all ages find it difficult, if not impossible, to analyze their feelings, and they grope with death's upheaval. Reaching out to your child is imperative.

As children grow, their psychological needs and understandings change. Thinking patterns, perceptions, and language development affect a child's ability to comprehend. Both your child's chronological age and his development may fall into the age group for cognitive thinking. Or he may still be in earlier thinking patterns, even though his age would indicate a different level of comprehension. Study the following stages of thinking and reaction patterns, so you can work effectively with your child's needs.

Magical Thinking Stage
(*Ages One Through Five*)

Children in the first stage or developmental group show the following characteristics:

1. Language confusion.
2. Fusion of real world and imaginary world.
3. Time confusion.
4. Perceive bad always magically changed to good.
5. Grief timetable different from adult's grief progression.
6. Unable to understand emotions.
7. Security threatened by family turmoil.
8. Thinking only in concrete concepts.
9. Hear words, but have little comprehension.

For children in this stage there is little separation between the real world and the world of imagination. Young children see dragons and imagine friends. The world is made of superheroes such as Mom and Dad, He-man, magical dolls that fly on ponies. Cartoon characters are real. When bad things happen, magic turns the evil into good. Daddy goes away in the car after breakfast, then magically returns home before dinner. When a sibling or friend dies, a child mentally equates it with Daddy's going away. He is gone for a while, but will come home. Dead things come back to life on television, in games, and in life, to the child on this cognitive level.

Children are befuddled by the confusion of death. They do not understand the disruption in their normal life activities. They do not understand the adults' grief, the many visitors, the disturbed routines. A child may sit in his game area, playing with trucks and cars, appearing unaware of the crisis around him. In reality, he may be experiencing strong disorientation. He may act casually to the news of the death, then days later begin crying desperately or acting out aggressively. Later, he will ask when the deceased child is coming home. "Where is my friend [my sister, my brother]?" He will not understand the answers about death. He will simply be confused.

In this stage the child will be far more affected by his sibling's death than a friend's death. His family is his base of security. When the pattern of behavior changes within the family, that threatens his whole base of security. If a close friend dies, the separation and the reactions of the adult world around him will confuse him, but he will quickly accept the separation as normal if his immediate world does not seem disturbed. This is not true for older children.

Death makes a child of any age feel vulnerable, but a young child will not know how to interpret these emotions. Sheer panic will clutch him; he will have a foreboding of being abandoned by others he loves. This perception of his world being out of control often causes a child to act out in negative behavior. In their studies, Bowlby and Parkes found that two-thirds of young children showed definite regressive behavior; one-fifth of the responding children were plagued with night terrors; one-fourth became excessively clinging to their parents; one-third acted out in aggressive and hyperactive behavior.[2]

Most young children show initial signs of grieving three to six months after the death. They do not begin to focus on the deceased child until their surrounding world seems normal again. Bereavement will manifest itself in whiny, frustrated, angry behavior. Then commences a pattern of questions, play acting, or confusion over words. Adults describe the child's behavior as bewildered, aggressive, fearful, or focused on playing "dead." He will ask hundreds of times when the deceased child can come back home, visit him, or play with him.

Children in this phase of thinking have no clear concept of time. *Today, tomorrow, three hours from now, forever, never* all mean nothing. Everything that happens is *now*. Everything that is going to happen is *tomorrow*. Everything that did happen is *today* or perhaps *yesterday*. To be gone for one hour when the child misses you is the same as having been gone forever. When you tell him his sibling will never come back again, he will ask if she can come home tomorrow.

Young children are confused by language. When we talked to our youngest child about the dangers of drowning, he confused the *death* of LeeAnne with *drowning* and *diving*—all *d* words. He had heard *dying*, and now we were using *dying* in relationship to the swimming pool, so that must mean LeeAnne died diving in the swimming pool. He could die, too. See, he died, just like LeeAnne, when he dived off the pool board. We could repeatedly explain that the death of his sister had nothing to do with diving or drowning, but the explanations bounced off his lack of experience, the way water drops off a tin roof.

Adult reasoning does not blend with a child's perception of reality. Though children hear the answers to their questions, they do not comprehend the meaning. Talk on the child's level of understanding. In trying to simplify the concepts, avoid phrases and images that lead the child to resent God for taking his sibling away—like the wicked wizard or evil villains in a fairy story.

Never do the following:

1. Refer to death as "sleeping."
2. Talk about God "needing" or "taking" his sister or brother or friend.
3. Imply it was "God's will" that the child died.

Your child may play dead, talk about dying, be consumed with death. Acting out what he hears or misunderstands is quite normal. His whole world has been filled with people crying, talking about his deceased sibling or friend, looking at pictures, reliving memories. Seeing shocked expressions or hearing commands to stop talking about dying or the deceased sibling will intensify his guilt and bewilderment. He needs to release his confusion through "playing" and "rambling random thoughts."

We knew our two-year-old was too young to understand his six-year-old sister's death. We were wrong. He has experienced deep grief. Brad's grief manifestations have been typical of a young child. He has dealt with confusion, deep yearning, anger, questioning, reliving the death—as he understands it.

Brad thought LeeAnne had gone in the car. After all, everyone who left our home went away via car, then returned again. He had not expressed much concern about where his sister had gone. Two months after her death, Brad was playing in a toy car outside. LeeAnne and Brad had played cars together, chasing each other, bumping, following the leader. He kept calling her name and asking us why LeeAnne didn't come home to play with him. This initiated a two-day whiny, crying, agitated, grief period for Brad.

After that brief period, he seemed to return to his normal behavior. But throughout the two years, these periods have come and gone. He has continued to ply us with questions: "Why don't we go to heaven and get LeeAnne?" "Why doesn't God bring LeeAnne back home?" "Is LeeAnne at her school?" "Can LeeAnne talk to us when we go to her classroom?" "Is this how LeeAnne died?" (as he dives to playact dying), "Can I die, too? I'll be back tomorrow."

He has played dead games. He has been afraid. He has told us, "I don't want to die. I don't want to go to heaven and be with God." He wants his sister to come home. He doesn't understand how her body can be at the cemetery, if she is in heaven. Our answers have been simple, repeated many times. Talking about LeeAnne has been natural, but he remains confused.

Though slightly older children may experience less confusion, they, too, will have limitations of understanding. What can you expect of a child between ages six and eleven? Let's see.

Self-centered Stage
(*Ages Six Through Eleven*)

Children in this stage show the following characteristics in understanding death:

1. Thinks in terms of concrete concepts.
2. No gray zones in morals—everything is "good" or "bad."
3. Friends are considered extended family.
4. Good not always seen as victor over evil.
5. Understands time concepts.
6. No degree of friendships, people are either "friends" or "enemies."
7. Feels threatened by his own emotions.
8. Language no longer confusing, unless dealing with abstract concepts.

The second stage is the most vulnerable one in which a child can experience the death of a sibling or friend: Language development and understanding of the cycles of life are greater; death is a reality, reinforced by the loss of pets and dead bugs. Yet the child still thinks in concrete concepts. In his mind, cause and effect answers the "whys" that emanate from a death. Since life is centered on *I,* he may rationalize that an action or inaction on his part caused or abetted the death.

As a child begins to feel himself separate from his parents, his mind fills with fears. Good no longer always triumphs over evil. Skeletons, ghosts, and haunting spirits terrorize the night. Monsters lurk in closets. Death can stalk, taking family and friends—or the child himself. There is a heightened feeling of vulnerability. Questions ring through a child's thoughts: *Where have they gone? Why have they gone? Will I die, too?* The last question, laden with fears for self, is the clincher, the main looming thought.

A friend's death can be as psychologically threatening as a sibling's, because children have begun to reach out to their friends, accepting them as part of their extended family. They have begun to share secrets, as well as activities. Friends have a forever understanding. At this age they become "blood sisters" or "blood brothers," using initiation rites and secret codes, forming cliques. Never do they consider that anything could separate such friends.

Grieving is manifested in fearful, regressive, clinging, withdrawn behavior. As the weeks pass, bereavement seems to end, only to appear again months later. Typically, about eight months after the child's death, his siblings or peers become consumed with anxiety. Preoccupation with the deceased child may be evident, though the only indication may be excessive insecurity. Unfortunately, this pattern of appearing to have accepted the death, then becoming consumed by fears or memories will continue until teenage years. As a child's abstract thinking expands and he begins to think philosophically, he ceases feeling so fearful. He begins to expand his vision, so that he is no longer the "center" and thereby "cause" of all that happens.

Most children will not talk openly about their feelings unless a parent opens the door to communication. Perhaps this is the first time a child has confronted the fact that someone he loves can be separated from him, and it does not conform to his sense of rightness. He is not mature enough to analyze emotions and reactions. Though he understands sadness, he feels other emotions—anger, aggressiveness, insecurity, fear, or resentment—occur because he has been "bad." Being guided in analyzing the reasons for feeling threatened and vulnerable can help a child accept his emotions as normal, not due to imperfection.

Because the child feels deprived of something important to

his life, death of a sibling or friend can cause anger. Subconsciously he feels hostility for the anguish and hurt he is encountering. He experiences feelings of rejection; his sibling or friend chose to leave him. (This line of reasoning follows the normal cause-and-effect thinking: *Because* I *did something wrong or bad. . . .*) Anger and rejection can lead to two extremely different destructive behaviors:

Aggressiveness acted out through misbehavior or violent outbursts.
Withdrawal and isolationism.

Before LeeAnne died, we had scheduled a Brownie end-of-the-year swimming party at our home. The party was to be one month after her death. When the leader called to give us the option to cancel, we chose to have the children come as planned. After the sixteen little girls arrived, I sat down with them. LeeAnne had been their friend. They needed to ask questions and to talk. They needed reassurances and answers.

Their questions were not hidden behind masks of tact: "Are you still missing LeeAnne?" "What are you going to do with her room?" "Do you think she is in heaven?" "Why did she die?" "Do you cry a lot?" "Do you want another little girl?" "Could we come over to visit?" "Did LeeAnne hurt when she died?" "Can I have a picture?" "Do you think she is missing us?"

Every child wanted to see LeeAnne's room. They all had the basic apprehension that we would forget LeeAnne; it rang with the fear that if something happened to them, would they be forgotten? We reassured them we would all remember LeeAnne, because she was sent by God to share her love with us for the almost-seven years she lived. There were favorite things of LeeAnne's we would always cherish, because they had been special to her. We would always miss LeeAnne, but we knew God was taking good care of her in heaven. Their questions were answered. More important, they were reassured that if death happened to them, they would not be forgotten.

LeeAnne had several very special friends, who have grieved deeply. Mary found it very difficult to return to school. She did not want to make close friends. She clung to her parents. Linda called us constantly, wanting to know how we were doing, what we were doing, could she come over? She has idealized LeeAnne to the point where no other friends compare. LeeAnne has become her imaginary friend.

All Lee's close friends have gone in and out of grieving. They appear fine, then months later have regressed to deep insecurity reactions—afraid for parents to leave, nighttime fears, not wanting to be away from home. Distant friends, even acquaintances, have followed a similar pattern. John compares all girls to LeeAnne—none are as great—neither are his boyfriends. Arron has made a "LeeAnne" corner in her room, with mementos of LeeAnne—a picture, a necklace, a ticket from the skating rink where they went together, a drawing.

For a child in the next stage, the reactions to death can be more subtle, perhaps more hidden, but he may be no less devastated.

Cynical-Idealistic Stage
(*Ages Twelve Through Twenty*)

Older children will show these characteristics in grieving:

1. Alternating between need to establish self-identity and desire for protection.
2. Thinking in concrete–abstract concepts.
3. Able to evaluate relationships.
4. Desiring support for his unique personality.
5. Body mature.
6. Idealistic or cynical approach to life.

7.   Vacillating self-esteem.
8.   Judgment limited by lack of experience.

When a teenager experiences the death of a brother, sister, or friend, his thoughts are very different from those of a younger child. He has already begun to deal with the issues of life and death, good and bad, afterlife, and independence. The way he reacts to the death will depend upon his own sense of security, his closeness to the deceased person, the support of his family, his religious beliefs, and his sense of life's purpose.

At first he will experience shock and disbelief. Then as he alternates between disbelief and acceptance, he will struggle with *why* questions. If the deceased was a sibling or close friend, he may withdraw from close relationships with others. Because the pain of losing a loved one is so intense, he cannot conceive becoming emotionally bonded again. Time is the key factor in a young person's overcoming this fear.

If death was caused by self-inflicted problems, such as suicide, drugs, or drinking, the youth will feel a potential victim, if he has been part of the activities. Added to his sorrow will be anxiety and a tinge of guilt.

If a youth has been raised to believe that God is in control of the world and life, he may surprise you with his acceptance of his sister's, brother's or close friend's death. He may focus on the positive value—the quality—of life, as opposed to the longevity. Yet for years his emotions will vacillate between acceptance and turmoil over the loss.

The most rewarding element of experiencing death at such a young age is a new awareness of the value of life. When you talk with teenagers, be aware that the death of a loved one or close friend is often the pivotal point for developing a sense of purpose. Death can make a teenager want to accomplish something, to share his limited time. It is a dramatic awakening to the shortness of life—and its fragility.

Many young people find it difficult to express their emotions of grief to parents. There are four basic reasons for this withdrawal reaction:

1. A desire to protect his parents from additional grief and burden.
2. Guilt.
3. The drive to be independent causes him to feel he must shoulder his own hurt, without help.
4. Lines of communication have been damaged.

Even if the youth seems to discuss the death openly with his peers, it is critical for parents to talk with the teen. Peers lack the life experiences that help them understand and evaluate tragedy. Youths yearn to discuss their anxieties, confusion, and frustration. They want to feel their parents are concerned enough to ask and listen, even when they outwardly reject the help. Parental love, approval, and guidance are needed more than ever after a death. After tragedy, children of every age regress in their need to feel sheltered and protected.

All relationships include ambivalent feelings (love versus hate, anger versus pleasure). Rarely does a young person have the experience to recognize and accept ambivalent feelings as normal. Adult guidance helps him understand that he needs to forgive himself for not being perfect within his thoughts or actions to his brother, sister, or friend.

Help your youth to focus on the uniqueness of the deceased child's life and guide him to understand that the quality of life is more important than its length. These awarenesses can affirm that every phase and point of life is to be enjoyed.

Like an adult, a youth can become stuck in the negative emotions of fear and anger. Depression is a serious outgrowth of death. At an idealistic stage of life, death can be a major jolt, bringing crushing reality into the picture. For many young people, already cynical from heavy problems, such as the divorce of parents, sex, and drugs, death merely confirms negative feelings. When life seems out of control and hopeless, death emphasizes the futility of plans and goals. These angry, bewildered emotions demand release. Partying, instant gratification, dropping out of goal-directed endeavors, suicide,

and challenging death through life-threatening activities can
become the negative outlets for these feelings.

We had two teenagers when LeeAnne died: Kim was nineteen, Paul was sixteen. Both coped amazingly well—too well.
Daddy Paul and I felt concerned that they were walling off their
emotions. We talked openly with them about LeeAnne, encouraged them to talk, involved them in the book I was writing,
asked their feelings. Yet both walked through the stages of
death, showing little outward effect. Not until almost a year
later did Kim allow her pain to break through her stored hurt.
It took Paul Edward almost two years.

For Kim the breaking point came when Daddy Paul and I
asked her to talk with us about adoption. We had a tremendous, aching loneliness for a child to fill the vacancy left by
LeeAnne. Kim was home for a college break. When we
discussed the possibility of adoption with her, the pent-up
emotions began to pour out like water.

Kim had run away from the reality of her sister's death by
filling her time with college activities. Facing the idea of
adoption forced her to realize LeeAnne's death was final. Her
emotional release was healthy. She had been too strong.
Though she had accepted LeeAnne's death as God's design
in her mind, she had not dealt with her aching emotions.

Paul Edward had a similar reaction. He had been a vital part
of LeeAnne's life, giving her shots, watching over her closely,
teaching her to water-ski, horseback ride, snow ski. They were
extremely close. Always our open, expressive child, after
LeeAnne's death Paul put a lock on his emotions. He rarely
showed anger, keeping his emotions under strong control.
Often he would watch the videos of LeeAnne; occasionally he
would tell of having a hard day with his remembrances of Lee.
These were his limited outward signs of grieving.

Like Kim, Paul Edward expressed deep faith in God's
design after LeeAnne's death. Faith meant acceptance.
Daddy Paul and I, even with trust in God's love, gave
ourselves permission to work through our anguishing emo-

tions. Both Kim and Paul also wanted to protect Mom and Dad from more hurt by display of their sorrow.

Paul Edward's release followed a tremendous load of pressure at school. He was under great stress, though he acted easygoing and relaxed. In all college-bound classes, he had a tough daily academic load. A teacher added to the strain, because she felt Paul was capable of an *A* in her class, though he was happy with a *C*. By daily verbal attacks in class she wanted to make him angry enough to prove his ability. His response was total calm—and resolve that he would do as little work as possible in her class. In addition, he was preparing for the state diving competition. He was top in his conference and had a good chance to be first in the state. It required daily hours of diving practice. He also was under pressure deadlines for college application.

On the night his reserve broke and the painful emotions escaped, we planned our first skiing trip since LeeAnne's death. The last major activity with LeeAnne had been a skiing trip. Paul Edward, her close companion on the trip, had helped her with technique, watched over her energy level, and felt proud of her. The remembrances, the pressures at school, and the stored emotions came bubbling to the top. He broke down and released his pain. Slowly he became open again in expressing his emotions, but the breaking-through point had released him from having to wall off his emotions.

Death is hard. It shakes youth's every foundation. Helping teens come through it with emotional health takes a great deal of effort. They may try to resolve their grief alone, but they can't. They need help!

Questions

About Children Ages One Through Five

My child talks about his friend's [or sibling's] death. He does not seem to be grieving. Should I talk with him about the death? Talk in small doses. If your child is touched by death, it is important that you help him understand his confusion about where the child has gone, why everyone is sad, why he died. Be honest about your emotions. Talk in concrete terms. "I miss her." "I like to picture God holding her on his lap." "I think she must be laughing and playing in heaven." "I am crying because I am sad."

The child will listen, then dance off. Thoughts and confusion are like a ball that keeps bouncing in his mind. He needs an adult to help him understand the tragedy. Without such help, he will interpret the negative emotions around him as something he has caused. Without adult guidance, the confusion meshes to produce insecurity.

Is this age too young to be involved with the funeral rites? Siblings six and up need to be part of the final rites. If the service is a closed-casket service, consider it for a four- or five-year-old friend. Siblings and friends under four should not attend.

Most funeral services and visitations involve open caskets, great sadness, and an overwhelming sense of tragedy. On a young child with limited understanding, the death of a child will have a negative impact. Years of fear and deep psychological problems surrounding death can grow out of being part of a tragedy at an emotionally fragile age. Even a young child accepts death more readily if the deceased is old.

We received a letter from a young woman who attended LeeAnne's funeral. Though we did not know her, she wrote to thank us for the positive service. Then the sad part of her letter began. Her closest childhood friend had died in an accident, and the funeral rites had devastated her. Her friend lay in the casket—without color, in a dress she remembered from fun times together, without expression, dead.

That woman recalled nightmares that became part of her life. She became shaky, withdrawn, tearful at even the thought of death rituals. However, the focus of LeeAnne's services as a farewell and thanksgiving for Lee's precious life had changed her perspective on death. It was positive, strengthening, not frightening.

Younger children can visit the family in their home, taking some food, a book, a picture. The visit provides an opportunity to talk about death without adding the confusion of rituals.

About Children Ages Six Through Eleven

How can I help my child with his fears? Provide him with schedules. Let him know what he will be doing, when he will do it, and where the rest of the family will be during these times. If you hand him a tangible schedule, he can cling to the reassurances that you will return. When it is impossible to meet a deadline, call to reassure him everything is okay.

Ease night fears by leaving a light on in the room, playing a tape or record, allowing him to sleep in a closer bedroom. Some nights he will need to sleep with you, but this won't go on forever. When he begins to feel less vulnerable, the need for such appeasements will vanish.

Since her friend's death, my child is overwhelmed with a need to be perfect. What can we do? To an adult, a child's logic may seem illogical. A deep-seated fear that if she isn't perfect in everything, she will die, follows her cause-and-effect reasoning. Help your child's growing understanding that many things are not in our control, nor do we have answers for many of the *whys* in life. We must trust God, who protects and guides our world.

Advise teachers of the underlying reason for the child's perfectionistic behavior. Adults need to reassure the child that love for her is unconditional, not something she must earn.

My child has made a shrine out of his deceased friend's picture and memento. Is this healthy? In the magical-thinking stage, children think their sibling or friend will magically reappear. Children in the self-centered stage are more realistic. Your child needs a tangible item with which to work through his inner turmoil. Such cherished objects become important because:

1. They give a child a focus on which he can direct his thoughts or talk out his feelings.
2. A memento can help alleviate the feelings of rejection. The child's rationalization: *If I have a treasure of my sibling or friend, he must still love me.*
3. Having something tangible to hold makes the death seem less final.

My child is concerned about her deceased friend's parents, and my reassurances do not quell her anxiety. Should I contact her friend's family? Death of a friend will be one of the greatest tragedies your child will handle. Do whatever seems logical to help her deal with the trauma. Invite the parents to visit, for dinner, or ask to visit them. Let your child be involved in preparations for the dinner or making or selecting a gift to take to the friend's home.

Two needs will be met by visiting with her friend's parents:

1. Reassurance that she has not been forgotten by the family of her friend.
2. The need to do something to be helpful for her friend's family.

Before the get-together, talk openly with the parents about your child's concern for their welfare. Share her longing for her friend. They will be deeply touched to know their child is not forgotten. Also, knowing you give permission for them to continue loving your child will be a cherished gift. Because of their deep grief, they may be unable to become part of the child's life again, but they will feel grateful to be remembered by him.

Why does my child seem so stunned by the death of a child in his school? They were not close. There is little differentiation between friendship levels at this age. A friend is a friend. If you are not a friend, you are an enemy.

Why does my child feel guilty about his friend's death? Guilt accompanies death. Because a child's world revolves around self, it is logical for him to wonder if something he did or failed to do caused his friend's or sibling's death. Degree of friendship has nothing to do with these feelings. He may feel guilty because he failed to kick a ball to the deceased child at the last recess period or did not say hello in the school hall or did not ask him to his birthday party three months before the death or got the bigger slice of apple pie at dinner.

My child is so whiny and negative since his friend's [or sibling's] death. Why? Rarely can a child in this self-centered stage verbalize his feelings, unless someone helps him. He understands language well, but is not mature enough to analyze his feelings and reactions. Children can respond to questions about why they feel sad after a death, but they do not know why they feel whiny, aggressive, resentful, or mad. Instead they equate these emotions with being "bad."

By being guided in the maturing process of analysis, a child can accept and come to grips with feelings that otherwise threaten and make him feel vulnerable. The props of his understanding of life have been knocked askew: Children, especially friends, do not die. He needs adult understanding to deal with such tragedy.

Almost two years ago my child's friend died. Yet I overheard him talking about his deceased friend as if they were still best friends. Does he need counseling? If your child has experienced the death of a sibling or close friend, he will vacillate emotionally for years. Whenever he is insecure, having problems in new relationships, or facing emotional lows, he will remember his friendship with deep longing. He

may be having no problems, but desires the idealized relationship he envisions. Perhaps having a perfect friendship
puts him higher on the totem pole of "I have's" when
discussing "self" with friends.

Don't try to talk him out of his remembrances by telling
him his friendship was not the perfect relationship he has
idealized. Through the years—and much talking—a child will
grow to understand realistic expectations in friendships.

If the idealization causes him to withdraw from other
friendships, professional counseling may be helpful. Fear of
losing another friend can become a wall that keeps the child
from establishing new friends.

About Children Ages Twelve Through Twenty

**Since his sibling's death, my child seems to be shouldering
the burdens of our whole family. What can we do to help
him realize he doesn't have to handle so much?** He may
be trying to compensate for being alive. Living, when your
sibling is dead, does not seem justifiable. "If only" wishes
plague the youth. There is a natural desire to "make it up" to
the parents. Often, sincere but misguided comments, such as,
"You'll have to help your parents, now that your brother has
died," are enough to afflict the living sibling for life.

A parent must be sensitive to his child's needs and must not
assume that because the child has returned to normal activities, all is well. He must open the door to communicating
about feelings, the stages, God, goals, and life. In addition he
must communicate to the youth that he is unique, a gift of
God, appreciated and loved. The child must know that he
need not compensate for his sibling's death or protect his
parents from his hurt.

What is my child's greatest fear since his brother's death?
After a death, the greatest fear of every teenager is that life
will never become happy again. He watches his parents with
trepidation. Life seems chaotic, out of control.

Positive Approaches

For Ages One Through Five

What helps a young child's progress through the stages of acceptance of a death?

1. Understanding his behavior and accepting it.
2. Using patience and love when answering his confused questions.
3. Answering questions, using sensitivity to his level of language understanding.
4. Building pictures in his imagination of his sibling or friend being loved and protected by God.
5. Helping him to feel his sibling or friend still loves him.
6. Using lots of positive body language—hugs, kisses, and holding.
7. Sharing with him why you are sad, crying, or depressed, so that he does not feel he is the cause of your anguish.
8. Using books like *Thumpy's Story*, by Nancy C. Dodge, to provide opportunities for your child to verbalize his feelings.
9. Using art—drawing or coloring—as an outlet and talk-through opportunity.
10. Adult playacting with the child, using dolls or puppets, to allow expression of his emotions.

For Ages Six Through Eleven

What helps a child of this age range progress through the stages of acceptance of a death?

1. Understanding that though the child seems more mature, he is unable to deal with death in a fully mature way.
2. Realizing that a child in this age group is far more vulnerable to feelings of guilt and insecurity than in either the magical-thinking or the cynical-idealistic stage.

3. Dealing with the child's fear and frustration, which come from his inability to analyze his own feelings and reactions.
4. Sharing ideas about heaven, God, and life's values and meaning in concrete concepts.
5. Providing a security blanket of protection and love around the child as he tries to move toward independence in his understandings.
6. Providing professional counseling if you find your child unable to cope with his fears and emotions after a death.

For Ages Twelve Through Twenty

What helps a teenager progress through the stages of acceptance of his friend's or sibling's death?

1. Sharing what to expect as one progresses through the stages of grief.
2. Through talking about your own feelings of loss, opening the door for the youth to talk about his emotions of grief.
3. Encouraging the youth to do something special for the family of the deceased—write a letter, mow the yard, bake goodies, baby-sit.
4. Being a support system.
5. Allowing the child to be part of the family decisions on types of funerary rites or object dispensation.
6. Discussing the spiritual parts of life—the value of life, life after death, God.
7. Accepting his emotions and responses without shock or negative reactions.
8. Sharing your emotions and turmoil, positive and negative responses, so that he feels you need his support.

Nine

If You Are a Friend _____

You are a friend of someone whose child has died. Available, eager, you search for any way possible to say, "I care." You want to be a support. Searching for the words to enhearten, to encourage, to inspire, you grope for ideas to soothe the pain and bring relief. Your mind ricochets with ways to strengthen your friends. But you don't want to do something wrong!

You are stymied. A wall of fear surrounds you, thwarting active moves to assist. Riveting questions bridle your attempts to help: *Will I be in the way? What should I say? If I become emotional, will it hurt them even more?*

You feel lost! Where are the guides? Who can tell you what to do? Will what you do be perceived as "help" or "intrusion"? You don't want to unintentionally add to the grief. To complicate the matter, you, too, feel a sense of grief. The deceased child had been part of your life.

There is another feeling, a feeling of guilt. *But for the grace of God, it could be my child*, echoes between thoughts. Why has your friend been cursed, while you have been spared? There you sit, wanting to help, feeling real grief for the child who has died, hurting for the parents, and twinging with guilt that your children are safe and well.

Quit struggling with the questions and concerns. You are desperately needed. Trust your instincts. You may be the key to your friend's survival. It *will* make a difference if you help.

Throw off the concerns about how your friends will react toward you. They need you, your love, and your compassion. They need to be hugged, cried with, listened to, and helped in a thousand small ways. Their state of shock barely allows them to function. On the inside they will not be judging your behavior or intact family. They scream for help, help to survive, courage to make it through the next hour.

Though they may seem calm, in control, and may verbalize succinctly, inside, they are dazed, disbelieving of their child's death, moving between agonizing reality and slow-moving denial. They need friends and family to be near, to shoulder and cushion the pain, to listen, to lament, to take the responsibility for details that give hospitality to visiting friends and family.

Two sets of distinctive needs follow death: needs prior to the funeral and needs after the funeral.

Before the Funeral

Goal: To shoulder the hospitality needs, leaving the family free to deal with their emotional crisis and the myriad of funeral details. If you are a close friend, make yourself indispensable. Answer the phone, take messages, call friends and acquaintances, accept flowers, clean up the house, keep food available for relatives, help with the other children in the family, iron clothes or, even better, coordinate the scheduling of friends to handle the multitude of hospitality jobs.

Assume the family wants your help. Though you will want to ask for specific job needs such as shopping and dry cleaning, don't expect the family to give directions. Anticipate the needs and quietly manage the tasks: mow the yard, wash the car, feed the dog, or run the vacuum. The family is too dazed to handle details. Worry about being in the way? No! If the family does not want help, they will tell you; most will be eternally grateful.

It is essential to keep a notebook of who brought what, who called, who visited, for even close friends' visits and significant kindnesses will fade into a blur for the family. Each visitor, each item of food, each call listed will testify that a friend or family member cared. The names will jog the foggy memories and prevent needless hurt. Anger in the bereaved has kindled for years because friends who came and cared were not remembered.

Friends took over the hospitality needs of our home when LeeAnne died. When we got home from the hospital, they were there. They answered the doorbell and the phone, brought in food, resupplied the kitchen paper goods, made a scrapbook of LeeAnne's pictures, cleaned up the dishes, turned off the lights at night, and reappeared to make coffee in the morning. Our extended family is large, so perhaps they could have carried the load. Instead they were free to talk and work through their own grief with us as we resolved the funeral choices.

A sister took pictures. Pictures? Yes! (We didn't want a bevy of emotion-laden pictures. A friend or family member was inconspicuous, present during many important times, sensitive, knowledgeable of the family members and friendships.) After the services, pictures awoke our beclouded memories of the flowers, casket, friends in the kitchen, visiting relatives, children playing in LeeAnne's room, men parking cars, the dog being groomed and the numerous other ways people shared their love with us.

Special Helps Prior to the Funeral:

1. Notify friends and acquaintances of the death.
2. Coordinate the helping activities.
3. Bring food in labeled or throw-away containers.
4. Return the dishes.
5. Baby-sit.
6. Help with clothing needs: shopping, ironing, dry cleaning, sewing.
7. Arrange housing for out-of-town guests.
8. Make a scrapbook of the deceased child's pictures, to place on the coffee table.
9. Arrange for the care of pets.
10. Take photographs if the family wants them.
11. Keep notebooks of visitors, food, flowers, and helpers.
12. Arrange for a housesitter during funeral services, to deter theft.
13. Be an answering service for the phone and door, keeping record of the calls and visits.
14. Call to inform friends and family of the details of the death and funeral arrangements.
15. Save the local newspaper announcement of the death.
16. Tidy up the house.

Following the Funeral Services

Goal: Emotional support for the family during the devastating months of emptiness that follow the burial.

The initiation into grief requires friends' physical presence to carry out the responsibilities. After the services, the key need is emotional support. How can a friend be a support?

Through visits, telephone calls, notes, invitations to one-on-one activities. Drop in to visit, with a book. Bring sweet rolls for breakfast. Call to check on grocery needs. Ask to take the children to a special activity. Invite them to go "with you" to social gatherings. (Going alone is horrendous.)

Don't say, *"Call me if you need me!"* You may mean it, but your bereaved friends will be unable to call for help. Grief takes away the ability to ask, because the pit is too deep to reach for light. Until the bereaved are strong enough to begin pulling themselves out of the emotional crypt, someone has to shine the flashlight into the dark.

Men, especially, need friends to reach out to them. Women tend to surround their women friends who are in pain. On the other hand, men become almost isolated. Their friends tend to avoid talking about the child and expect the bereaved father to handle his emotions. The most common comment a man hears is "How is your wife doing?"

Don't be embarrassed if someone shows you his or her hurt. You haven't caused him additional wounds. You have allowed her to vent anxiety and loneliness. It's sad to hear friends say, *"Oh, I'm so sorry. I didn't mean to bring something up that would cause you painful memories."* Memories are all the family has left, and they want to remember. They beg to remember and cherish friends who allow reminiscence.

As your friend leans on you, reassure him that it is good to show emotion. Let him know that emotion does not mean his faith is weak; it shows he is human and needs God's undergirding strength. Allow him to vent his anger against whatever or whomever; you don't need to defend those toward whom he directs the anger. He speaks from anguish, not reason.

Some believe the sooner the stricken parents forget their grief and go on with life, the better off they will be. They outline a timetable for the bereaved and set guidelines for his emotions. However, God has established a slow and laborious healing plan. Rushing the process has disastrous effects:

divorce, social alienation, preoccupation with the deceased, drunkenness, or hostility.

As a friend, you are needed for support and comfort, yes, and guidance. You are *not* needed for correction, reprimands, or control. You want to help your friends survive the time required for healing. If they become bogged down in the choices for recovery, you want to lend an extra hand. You may be the factor that prevents one tragedy from becoming a multiple tragedy!   .

Guidelines for Friends

Once the services are over, friends may have a hard time knowing just what to do or say. Here are a few basic dos and don'ts and some answers to the questions most people have.

Do

1. Listen.
2. Allow your friends to cry.
3. Express your own emotions and sadness.
4. Be encouraging, hopeful, and knowledgeable that God is surrounding the family.
5. Encourage your friends to be patient with their emotions.
6. Let your friends know their faith is no less because their emotions are askew.
7. Help them understand the stages of grief.
8. Aid them in realizing each family member will show grief in a unique way.
9. Equate strength with surviving, not holding back the emotions.
10. Give special attention to the living brothers and sisters.
11. Reassure the family that they loved and were good to the deceased child.

12. Refer to the child by name.
13. Share that healing takes time.

Don't

1. Be shocked by anger statements.
2. Try to justify the death.
3. Point out that they have other children or that they can have another child.
4. Try to find something positive about the death, such as closer family ties or a moral lesson.

What Do You Say?

When a child dies, friends feel confused and tongue-tied, because they don't want to hurt the family. Say: *"I'm so sorry." "We are going to miss _____" "I hurt for you." "I want to tell you something that will always be so special to me about _____." "I love you." "I don't understand 'why,' but it does comfort me to know _____ is being protected by God right now." "Tell me what happened." "I can only begin to understand the hurt you are feeling. How are you today?"*

Many children die after a prolonged illness. Never suggest that the child is now "better off." Say: *"I am glad _____ will not have to suffer anymore, but I am going to miss that little fellow."* Follow the remark with reasons his personality will leave a void in your life. Your remarks are being made to a bereaved family in the throes of peaking emotions, not reason. They aren't thinking why the child may be "better off." They are hurting, stunned, disbelieving, and desperately aching for their child.

We will always remember the friends who through anecdotes shared special characteristics of LeeAnne's personality with us. How desperately we wanted to know her life was not going to be forgotten, that it counted.

Make simple statements about God. The bereaved want to believe there is a God, because it means their child continues to exist. Even in the midst of hostility toward a God who would allow such a mistake, they want you to affirm that God cares, because the belief gives hope.

Don't argue the statements. Don't try to change anger. Affirm the care of God without suggesting God is responsible for the child's death, by saying: *"God loves you. He hurts for your pain." "God is taking care of _____. He won't let him feel alone." "I'm glad to know there is life after death, so we can be with _____ again someday."*

What do you do when you are asked, "Why?" Say, *"I don't know!"*

Are There Wrong Ways to Express Feelings?

Yes! Concern about what to say is legitimate. There are right and wrong ways to express feelings after a death.

One of the greatest examples of friends opening mouth and inserting foot is in the Bible. In the Book of Job, Job's three friends sat with him, wailing, in deep grief for seven days. After that period of time, they were tired of mourning; it was time for life to continue. The first seven days they supported Job; the next days they laced their words with criticism and judgment, justified by the motivation to "help" Job get back on his feet. Even God reprimanded the friends for their lack of understanding.

How do you help without causing more hurt by your remarks? When talking to the bereaved, throw out every phrase that rings with justifying the death or telling the bereaved how to grieve.

Avoid lecture statements. Though they may not say them, if you make comments like the ones below, the family will have the following thoughts.

"God loves you." (*He does?*)

"God must have had a reason." (*No reason justifies my child's death!*)

"You have to trust God's will." (*Why?*)

"Pray for peace and acceptance." (*I'll never feel peace again.*)

"God must have needed your little girl." (*I needed her, too.*)

"Won't she be a beautiful angel?" (*I wanted her to be a child.*)

"She'll never hurt again." (*Of course not! She's dead! She's dead!*)

No one adjusts to a child's death. No one considers death a real possibility, even when it lingers overhead for months. To consider the end of a child's life means you have given up hope. Giving up hope equates with failing your child. Avoid comments that indicate adjustment has been easier because of time to accept the possibility of death.

One young woman confided in me the reason I seemed to be coping so well. "Weren't you lucky? You had three days to accept LeeAnne's death before she was gone. It gave you time to work through your grief, didn't it?"

What could I say? "Yes, I was lucky. Gee, you are right, those days really made me willing to see her die." With disbelief that someone could make such an ignorant statement, I simply said, "I'm sure it helped." The woman had no children. She was steeped in our culture's "instant and throw away" attitudes. She had not gone through the experience. It wasn't her fault she was so naive. Lucky? I wanted to die!

Because of the way our culture views handicaps and disease, many people implied our adjustment was easier because LeeAnne had diabetes. After all, she wasn't a "normal" child. That was true; she wasn't normal: She was a blessing and a gift around which we totally wrapped our lives.

A ten-year-long disease culmination hurts as much as a totally unexpected death. In fact, the bonding when your child needs you so critically, as in cancers, diabetes, or arthritis makes freedom seem more poignant. The "free time," the sudden lack of being critically needed by the child, is a devastation, not a release.

Avoid element-of-truth statements. Some statements have an element of truth or may be completely true, but don't say them. Truth works for the reasoning power, but when your child dies, you become a sealed package of catastrophic emotions.

"There are things worse than death." (*Certainly. But not when you bury your child.*)

"At least you have other children." (*Children are not interchangeable.*)

"You are young. You can have other children." (*Maybe. But our dreams for this child are shattered.*)

"You had better be glad. Miscarriages mean something was wrong with the baby." (*Does this make me love my baby less?*)

"Someday you will look back and know you have grown from this tragedy." (*Maybe. Or this may be the beginning of a bitter, tragic life. Even if it eventually becomes true—which we all hope— a person on a hayride will not appreciate that rain makes the grass grow.*)

"I know this is tough, but let me tell you about another friend of mine. He lost two children. He really had a hard time!" Or, "Losing a child is hard, but when your husband or wife dies, it is even worse." (*You don't understand.*)

"Maybe you and your husband will be closer now." (*Closer? He's so wrapped up in his own grief and anger that he doesn't talk to me at all, now that our child is gone.*)

"There are so many problems in this life—drugs, sex, crime. He might have been a heartache to you later." (*I would have been willing to take the risk.*)

"I have always thought the best time to die was when you were young, before you became disillusioned with life or had major problems." (*That's because you haven't lost someone you love to death.*)

"After such a terrible accident, I bet the insurance companies had to pay through their noses." (*Gasp!*)

Avoid emotion-approval statements. Statements that tell the bereaved how to express their feelings or imply showing emotion is weakness are negative. If they are not allowed to get the pain out, it will destroy them. Weakness, no! It takes guts to show your deep emotions in our culture.

Avoid saying: "Be strong." "You have to hold up for the sake of your family." "It's time for you to pull out of this depression." "You can't go around angry. It is only hurting you." "This will pass." "You have to remember that our children are only loaned to us by God!" (*OUCH!*)

How Can I Help?

How long will my friends grieve? The length of time is as varied as the individuals. Count on intense grieving lasting a full year. Less intense grief will continue at least one more full year. Then grieving as such may be buried, surfacing periodically to throw pangs of hurt for the rest of life.

What is support for my bereaved friend: acceptance of her behavior, encouragement to "get out" of her grief, what? Acceptance and love are critical, but so is guidance. A friend visited me. She said, "Betty, this is what you can expect: You are going to find it hard to think. Your emotions are going to be helter-skelter. You will be sick. You will lose weight, then gain, no matter what you eat. You will feel insecure, crazy at times, in physical anguish and emotional mayhem. You'll be angry at those you love, maybe even God. Your focus will be on LeeAnne day and night. Life will return with happiness again, but that will take time, lots of time. I'm here for you, however; I'll keep checking on you, because you will find it hard to call for help."

Her words resonated through my mind as each statement played out in my life. Each comment reassured me that I wasn't different. I was experiencing normal grief. I was grateful for her guidance.

Friends allowed us to continue talking about LeeAnne. What a blessing! They didn't act shocked, uncomfortable, or embarrassed. The need to talk about your child eventually subsides. But at first, the emptiness and yearning drive every thought to him so that if you are not free to talk about your loss, the emotions fill and break the thin crystal of your emotional stability.

When the bereaved carry a load of guilt about the deceased, they tend to lock up their feelings. If you are able to gently help them release their guilt through reassurances and anecdotes of good memories of the child, you may save a major scar. Negative feelings must be released if peace is to return to the grieving parents. Keep focused on their grief, not on the way they will feel toward you. You are not invading their privacy. You would show your concern if the experience were a happy one, such as a wedding. It is needed even more in a death.

The bereaved walk an emotional tightrope. If they slip or cling perilously, come to their aid. Though you want to be accepting, be willing to reach out when you see your friends slipping into danger. Their whole family may be in jeopardy. Share your concern for them, if they are caught in any of the problems listed below.

1. Stuck in a stage.
2. Hooked on drugs to kill the emotional pain.
3. Rejecting their living children's needs.
4. Transferring anger to their spouse.

My bereaved friends seem to discourage our friendship. They never want to visit, call, or get together for fellowship. Are they angry at me? Maybe. Anger as a grief reaction can strike God, friends, or family. Perhaps your friends feel you did not respond to their need, said the wrong thing, or were not supportive. On the other hand, you may be interpreting their inability to reach out to others, lack of desire to be social, pining, and emotional chaos as aimed at you. These emotions cocoon the bereaved, making it almost impossible to pull out of the feelings of insecurity, guilt, and depression.

Be patient. Continue to be a caring friend, through phone calls, mini-visits, and invitations. If they react in anger, time will begin to heal the wounds. If they yearn for their child, your friendship is needed to help fill the void. After all, who should understand their grief better than a friend?

My friend keeps asking me, "Why?" What can I say? Say, *"I don't know."* He isn't really wanting your answer. He doesn't think you know. The depth of tragedy is so great, he doesn't believe even God could justify the death. If you give religious clichés or positive-thinking justifications, expect strong rebuttal. He can't understand the tragedy. Neither can you. Say so!

I know it is nice to bring food to the home after a death. How much? What kind? Food acts as a tension release to family and friends who visit the family after a death. It gives nourishment, a topic of conversation, a focal point for activity, a way to show support. Huge quantities of food seem to magically disappear.

Finger foods, casseroles, easy-to-store foods are best. Commonly many out-of-town guests spend most of the day with the family. Therefore, in addition to main-course dishes, breakfast supplies are needed: cereal, sweet rolls, and fruits. Staples such as sugar, coffee, and milk are critical. Paper and plastic products, paper plates, napkins, towels, utensils, cups and glasses are appreciated by the cleanup crew.

If possible, put food in disposable containers. If not, label your dish and be responsible for getting it again. We had a labeled dish for a full year before I had the courage to return it. The dish became symbolic to me of "the end." I could not deal with the emotions of returning it, of talking about LeeAnne's death and how we were surviving.

Why is it important to keep a record of phone calls and visitors? Though the family may seem calm, it is a mask that covers their state of shock. Memory will be hazy at best. Both visitors and phone calls will come when the family is not available, so in a notebook keep record of the caller's name, telephone number, and relationship to the family or deceased—such as Jodi Ferris, 289-1998, first-grade Sunday-school teacher.

How do I help the father deal with his grief? Rarely do men discuss feelings, emotional needs, or problems. Most relationships are centered around activities such as watching a ball game or playing tennis. After the death of his child, a father will hunger to talk through his overpowering emotions. He aches for release through expressing feelings with male friends. Allowing the hurt to show is difficult in a society that equates strength with control over emotions. If male friends can affirm the rightness of sharing his hurt, the sanction gives stronger permission than a woman's sanction.

Reach out to the father. Break through his facade of strength. Don't be stopped by his clichés. Inside he is being torn apart. Let him know you appreciate his ability to share his feelings. Express appreciation for his strength to persevere in the midst of inconceivable pain.

The funeral is over. Do my bereaved friends need to be alone? Most friends are emotionally drained after the days surrounding the funeral. They pull back and return to the responsibilities of their homes and families. This period rings with emptiness and the sinking reality for the bereaved. They need friends now, more than ever.

The first few days following the services seem unbearable. I thought I might go out of my mind. The pain I felt in the quietness threatened my sanity. I endured the agony because of caring friends. Their visits were short, yet each one gave me a little more strength to continue. Each topic of conversation was a reprieve from dealing with the full thrust of my hurting emotions. Making it alone is tough!

Can the family be enough support to pull one another through the crisis?   Rarely! The typical scenario within two years following a child's death is a family in the throes of destruction. The marriage collapses; the children have deep psychological problems; the parents are emotional wrecks. This tragedy demands outside involvement for most families to survive.

I'm not a close friend, but I would like to help. What can I do?   *Write a letter.* Letters with memories—or letters stating "I am thinking about you"—mean a lot. Marty, the school crossing guard, wrote us, sharing a memory of LeeAnne. LeeAnne had walked to school, dressed in a yellow dance tutu, ballet shoes, and tiara. As Marty held the waiting cars at bay, Lee danced across the street, twirling and pirouetting. In the middle of the street, she curtsied to the waiting cars, then bounced on to school. LeeAnne had brightened the day of each person who had watched her carefree performance. The letter brought us immeasurable joy.

Another acquaintance had not known LeeAnne. He wrote to share his appreciation for the celebration service in her honor. Frank shared how he had been touched by the comments of others about LeeAnne. His view of life was changed by the realization of the way our lives intertwine with others. We were warmed by his letter.

You might also offer to help with thank-yous, telephone to check on the family, visit, offer to baby-sit, do small things to show you care (mow the lawn, take a loaf of bread to the home, invite the family to dinner, wash the car, or walk the dog).

Tears well in my friend's eyes when we reminisce. Am I hurting or helping by bringing up the memories?   The tears that fill the eyes may be gratitude and appreciation for someone who is unafraid to mention the child's name. Whether of gratitude, memories, or loneliness, the tears are close to the surface. A caring friend allows the release of pent-up feelings by being willing to listen and understand.

How do I refer to the deceased child?   Refer to him by name. Refer to the child as dead. Do not talk of his being a precious angel, a cherub, asleep, cradled in God's arms, or gone away. Sidestepping reality is far more painful than simply hearing the truth. Couching the child's death in verbal palliatives denies the parents the opportunity to talk with you seriously. You signal death is difficult for you to handle. Therefore they avoid sharing their true feelings.

It is easier to deal with statements such as, "I am sure Janie is having trouble in school because of her brother's death," than, "I am sure Janie is having trouble in school because of her 'history'" (meaning her brother died).

My friend is guilt ridden. What can I do?   Since perfect relationships exist only in our dreams, some guilt is justified. As a friend, be reassuring that his searching questions are normal because of the great emptiness from his child's death. Recall good memories and self-giving characteristics you saw in him toward his child.

Some forms of death create additional burdens of guilt—deaths from accidents, child abuse, murder, or suicide (*see* chapter 11). Anger at the circumstances of the tragedy and the inability to have prevented it mesh into a wire netting that chokes positive responses. A friend needs to share God's forgiveness with his grieving friend. Release comes when the bereaved accepts God's forgiveness and forgives himself.

One overlooked aspect of guilt is that it is a gift from God. Guilt allows us to reevaluate our priorities and choices; it allows introspection, a focus on "self" improvements.

I think everything is going well for my friends, then they seem caught again in grief. What is wrong?   We think the stages of grief are a defined course, but stages are general routes. At his own rate of speed, each person travels through, skips, lingers, becomes stuck, and returns to any point in the progression. Staging is descriptive, not definitive.

Friends need to keep three considerations in mind:

1. If your friend is stuck in a stage, he may need an outsider's help to find the way out.
2. Sometimes the bereaved needs permission to return to happiness. He feels disloyal to his deceased child if he appears too happy.
3. Flipping in and out of stages may frighten the bereaved.

My friend talks about her deceased child as if he had been perfect. It bothers me. Should I remind her that her son was really quite normal? Idealization is normal. It hurts no one, with two exceptions. If it has become a comparative scale by which the parents judge the other children in the family, idealization can destroy them. If idealization arises from deep-rooted guilt, it can destroy the individual. A guilt-ridden person may need psychological counseling to free himself. Suggest a specific counsellor.

To help the children whose sibling has died, you must uphold the value of the deceased child's life, while sharing the unique personality characteristics of the living children. Tearing down the idealized child will force the parents to elevate the pedestal higher. Gently guide them away from comparisons. No one can compete with the dead.

My bereaved friend is leaving his wife and job. Should I try to stop him? Yes! Emotions direct most people after life-rending tragedy: *I can't stand this pain any longer. I just want out!* Unfortunately, the change won't stop the pain. It creates more coping problems.

"Out" may be the eventual outcome, but as a friend, try to stop it. Encourage the family to not make any life-changing decisions for one full year. Help them understand their

reactions. Suggest counseling. If the emotions can be sub-
jected to reason, there is hope for the family's survival.

**Our families have been close through the years. Can we
do something special to say "We care!"?**   Use these ideas
to communicate your love:

1. Plant a special tree on the family property.
2. Make a scrapbook of pictures your family has taken
    through the years, to give to your friends. Include pictures
    of members of your families sharing happy moments.
3. Frame a photograph of the child, from your photo collec-
    tion. This can become a treasured gift.
4. Write a letter sharing what the child's life meant to you.
    Your memories could become precious to your friends.
5. Frame a picture of the deceased child to hang among your
    own pictures. Knowing you still remember and continue
    to care for their child will be greatly appreciated by the
    bereaved.

Friends who care deeply and use these ideas in this chapter
to support the grieving family have done them a great service.
Without such people, a family may indeed not make it at all.
Don't underestimate the influence you could have on helping
your friends move beyond grief into wholeness.

Ten

A Word to the Wise _____

Friends are not the only ones who seek to help a family.
   Three types of professional care givers, doctors, nurses, and ministers, have unique roles in helping us deal with the tragic death of a child. Each has the opportunity to help or to create additional pain.

Doctors

Most children are pronounced dead in a hospital, and doctors usually bear the tragic news. It is important that they focus on three realities:

1. There is *no* easy way to be told your child is dying or dead.
2. To a parent, no amount of brain damage, limb damage, paralysis, illness, or burn will justify the child's death.
3. The doctor's presentation can make a significant difference in the family's initial acceptance of their child's death.

I am the wife of a doctor and have a great deal of respect for the medical profession. Most are genuine, caring individuals. It is easy to agonize with them when they face the tragic death of a young person. As a parent, I also sat on the side of the bed, waiting for the verdict. I know some doctors handle the situation far better than others. The neurosurgeon who cared for LeeAnne was a gem. You could feel his hurt for her—and his caring for us. He never presented the full tragic reality of her situation in one thrust. He gave us time. "We'll watch." "Things don't look good, but let's just wait and see."

Another physician examined Lee and let us know: "She's blind. She'll never be able to talk again. She probably will be a vegetable. The pressure must have blown most of her brain." He was painting the truth. She might have died at any moment, so he wanted to help us face reality. My reaction? *No! You don't know. She can recover. Children bounce back. You are leaving God out of your picture. No!*

My response was the same as when, panic stricken, I took twelve puppies into the veterinarian. The six-week-old, healthy-looking animals were having convulsions from worms. The mother dog had not been wormed before she became pregnant, so she passed the vermin to the pups. The vet looked at the puppies and assured me they would all die. My backbone straightened. *No way!* They would not die. I would help them live. Bottle-feeding, medicine-giving Nurse Betty came to the rescue. I fed the babies every hour around the clock, and only two of the litter died.

No question, we needed to face reality about LeeAnne's condition—but not reality without hope.

Lee's pediatrician arrived early the third morning. Obviously he had not slept well. He sat with us, hurting, shaking his head, "I just don't know. I just don't know what else we can do." I wanted to hug him and let him know it was all right. God would have to handle this problem. Why wasn't I angry that he couldn't find a solution? Because I knew he was trying. He was almost in tears. He was quiet, taking time to let us know he felt our suffering.

Parents know. I didn't want to admit it; I would not have given up until the moment she died. But we knew. Paul and I didn't discuss the possibility of death. Paul knew in his mind—but not his emotions. He went to the office the three days Lee lay in coma, frantically trying to keep up with his duties. Why? Because he thought she might be coma bound for months. He wanted to be free to be with her, if the situation worsened. The situation could hardly have been worse, but we refused to look at the facts. She was our baby. She would not die. She was being held by the machines; yet with all good signs weakening we could see her getting better each hour.

Doctors, please:

1. Be calm. Do not come out of doors, loudly pronouncing, "It is all over!" Don't hit and run.
2. Talk slowly and compassionately. The minutes you take now may save hours of psychiatric care and anger later.
3. Refer to the child by name.
4. Let your emotions show. Don't be stoic. God knows you hurt for this anguish. Don't hide it.
5. Share details of the death. The two greatest concerns will be "Was my child in pain?" and "Was my child afraid?"
6. Allow the family to be with the child when he dies—if possible.
7. Touch the parents: on the arm, hand, with a hug.
8. Offer the option of organ donations.
9. If an autopsy is needed, explain the procedure carefully.

Parents want reassurance that their child's body will be handled with respect.

10. Don't be frightened by a family's runaway emotions. Let them vent. Nothing in life will be so tough to handle!

11. Don't offer rationalizations about the child's death. "Your child would never have been normal . . . would have suffered . . . was too hurt to live." No parent feels "lucky" that his or her child died.

12. Don't offer coping advice: "Stay busy." "Have another child." "Count your blessings." Deal with the moment.

13. Don't offer medication. You will delay the grief process's natural healing.

Nurses

LeeAnne stayed in intensive care only three days. Some children are hospital bound for extended periods of time. Nurses become the most critical care givers to these children and their families. Certainly there is a need for confidentiality between the doctor and the nurse, and the doctor needs to handle explanations of the child's condition. But parents, as well as the child, need the nurses' caring concern.

Nurses, please:

1. Refer to the child by name.

2. Talk to the parents in reassuring ways. They will not automatically assume that the medical team is doing their best to help the child.

3. Help the parents feel part of the team, not in the way. They are frightened of their child's condition and afraid of the medical paraphernalia. But this is their child. Let parents parent.

4. Take pictures of newborns who die. The family will be grateful.

5. Be patient. Fear blocks understanding. Parents in distress may absorb little of what they hear.

6. Never say, "This is not the way I would handle this

problem." The parents must trust their child's medical team.
7. Even if the hope is only a glimmer, offer it.

Ministers

Ministers, the third care givers, have a difficult role. How devastating to be a representative of God's love to a family in the throes of grief for a child! Love? They see only their child, dead. Where was God anyway? It is no wonder that less than 25 percent of all ministers have the courage to visit the family even once after a death.

Ministers, you are needed as desperately as the physician. If you can keep two keys in mind, your caring will be accepted as comfort.

> After a death, you are viewed by the family as a representative of God, never just a person.
> The family needs spiritual guidance, regardless of their anger at God.

No question, you would like to be "just a person" at such a time. But you aren't, anymore than the physician is "just one of the guys." The timing requires your professional guidance. You must support the family in ways that do not turn their remaining trust into anger. Mini-visits give the family opportunities to vent their emotions while feeling the support of their church and God.

For the family, reentering the church can be one of the most difficult steps after tragedy. Your mini-visits can be the encouragement needed to make that move. Also, you can alert church members to specific needs of the bereaved. Trying to stand alone among people who know your pain is difficult.

Ministers, please:

1. Visit—many times. This will be an important factor in the family's healing.

2. Pray—each time. In prayers, thoughts can be said that will plant a seed.

3. Let the family members vent, without feeling any need to justify God's position, explain away their anger, or criticize their grief expression.

4. Talk in understandable, concrete terms about what to expect in grief.

5. Never try to explain why or justify the child's death. Simply keep throwing out thoughts of God's care for them and protection of their child.

6. If you see danger signs of the family member being stuck in a stage or the family falling apart, be caring enough to point them out. An outsider may be needed to prevent the one death from becoming a multiple tragedy.

Until the end of the nineteenth century, people died at home surrounded by family and neighbors. The hygiene may not have been the best, but the spiritual and emotional support were stronger than in our isolating, sterile hospitals. Today we have turned over the responsibility for support to the care givers: doctors, nurses, and ministers.

That places a lot of responsibility on shoulders already burdened with other duties. It also provides an opportunity to be a link to emotional stability for someone. God grants care takers who must struggle through the tragedy of a child's death the most precious of gifts: the gift to know your life has made a difference. Like precious china, the bereaved are fragile: Handle with care.

Eleven

Death's Vehicles _____

Let's look at the facts about children's deaths.

- Due to the increase in death from accidents, murder, and suicide, the trend toward longer life expectancy for a newborn has shown no increase since 1982.[1]
- While all other age groups are becoming healthier, the number of deaths among teens has risen 11 percent in the last ten years.[2]
- Epidemic diseases such as polio, measles, and chicken

pox, which used to cause waves of death in children, have been eradicated. Now, when a young person dies in America, the chances are three out of four that his death will be the result of violence: 53 percent from vehicular accidents, followed by suicide, drownings, burns, poisons, falls, and choking.[3]

• Accidents are the number-one cause of death in all American children, until the age of fifteen. The leading cause of death of white youths between ages fifteen and twenty-four is suicide; among black youths the leading cause is homicide.[4]

Suicide

• A youth commits suicide every ninety minutes in America.[5]
• The United States teenage suicide rate has risen 300 percent in the last twenty-five years, surpassing Japan and Sweden.[6]
• Suicide is the sixth leading cause of death between ages five and fourteen, second leading cause of death between ages fifteen and nineteen, main cause between ages twenty and twenty-four.[7]
• White males account for two-thirds of the suicides; they commit suicide five times more often than white females, ten times more than black females, two times more than black males.[8]
• Suicide among white male youths has increased in ages fifteen through nineteen by 61.3 percent and 44.8 percent in ages twenty through twenty-four years in this decade.[9]
• Nevada and New Mexico have the highest youth suicide rates, followed by Wyoming and North Dakota. Suicide for the western states is generally higher than in the rest of the country, except for Florida and Vermont.[10]
• Suicide has seasons, too. It peaks in the spring, specifically

April in the United States, May and June in England. In the United States there is also a peak around the holiday season of Christmas and the New Year.[11]

- School records indicate most youths who commit suicide are high achievers, perfectionists with high performance in academics and sports; therefore, it is not surprising that the suicide rate among college students is significantly higher than among the same-age youth not at college. Perhaps because of the high self-expectations, most did not seek available psychological counseling.[12]
- The suicide rate among teenagers and young adults is highest where these individuals have themselves lost a parent through illness or accident when they were young.[13]
- Seventy-two percent lived in a single-parent family.[14]
- One-third of suicide victims are legally intoxicated.[15]
- Most carried out standard "farewell" rituals before they took their own lives: giving away prized possessions, writing letters, or visiting special people.[16]
- Youth suicide tends to breed more suicide, as seen throughout our country in the clusters of suicides that break out after a suicide.[17]

Murder

- Every twenty-four minutes a victim of violent crime dies.[18]
- Murders have tripled in the last fifteen years.[19]
- The largest percentage of child homicides is of children under the age of one, killed by parents or family friends, and of children ages fifteen through nineteen, killed by stranger. Murder in both age groups has doubled in the last decade.[20]
- Blacks have almost five times as many homicides of children as whites. However, their rate of homicide has dropped almost one-third in the teenage group, while

white teenage homicide has almost doubled in the past decade.[21]

- Over 100,000 people are reported missing each year. The majority never found are children and teens. Homicide is suspected, though unable to be proven in most cases, because no body is found.[22]

Infant Deaths

- Each year, approximately 40,000 United States infants die before reaching their first birthdays. The latest statistics show the infant mortality rate was 18.4 per 1,000 live-born black infants and 9.4 per 1,000 live-born white infants.[23]
- One in seven fetuses spontaneously aborts (miscarries) in the first twelve weeks (approximately 15 percent); once fetal heartbeat is established, the spontaneous abortion rate drops to 3 percent.[24]
- Sudden Infant Death syndrome (SIDS) kills approximately 10,000 American babies each year. It kills more infants between the ages of one week and twelve months than any other disease and ranks second only to accidents as the cause of death in children between one week and fifteen years of age.[25]
- SIDS has a unique age distribution: a peak incidence between the first and third months of life, rare occurrence during the first month and after the fifteen month. It has a ratio of 3.2 male-to-female death rate; ratio among nonwhite infants of almost four times the death rate as in white infants, considered due to low-birthweight babies. Decrease of incidence occurs in the summer months, with peak of deaths occurring in the late fall.[26]
- No reliable statistics are available on the number of children who die as a result of child abuse; however in the last decade reported cases of child abuse have risen almost 200 percent.[27]

Grief Reactions

Formula for recovery after a death:
Way of Death + Variables = Reaction
Death + Reaction = Focus
Focus + Choice = Potential Recovery

Some ways of death, even a child's death, are easier. The way a child dies makes a difference. The beginning of grief is the same, and the end, the "letting go," has to be the same, but major components of the death package—guilt, emotional intensity, out-of-control feelings, and anger—are interwoven with how death claimed the child. Why? Because we react dramatically to the way death comes. Our minds fill with instant questions about the death, questions dealing with pain, guilt, and terror. This immediate subconscious response affects our focus; focus affects our potential recovery.

The amount and kind of support given and needed after a child's death is subconsciously controlled by our reaction to the way the child died. The way of death can affect how quickly we offer help, how long we continue comfort, and how willing we are to accept and seek support. Tragically the ones who need the most upholding to survive often receive the least because of an innate repulsion to the form of death, as in murder. That fact may never change, but your understanding may enable you to reach out with more empathy to those who may receive little support.

Let's look at the particular problems inherent in the way of death:

Murder

Murder brings terror, outspoken anger, shock, outrage, and immediate public support. All want to help and know the full, nauseous details of the death. Within the community, the stunned horror at the ugliness, the unfairness, changes to anger, revulsion, and withdrawal of help. Few want to be part of a scene that involves police, devastating anger, and a shattered picture of the "good life."

The family is devastated by the loss of their child and rage at the villain. Memories of the child are sublimated to visions of the brute violence of her death. Fantasies of the child's screams, pleas, and cries for help block sleep and the return to the duties of life. The invasion of the police couples with the complexity of the justice system to keep emotions peaked. Grief usually remains "on hold" for years as families seek revenge for the tragedy. Murder creates aloneness for the family.

The news coverage of the murder of a child in Pennsylvania chilled our nation. In hopes of providing positive identification of a four-year-old murdered child, parents of a missing boy were asked to listen to tapes of little boys being sexually brutalized to death. They listened, stunned, numb until they heard the screams of their own precious child, pleading for the pain to stop, for his mommy and daddy. The screams destroyed the family.

Suicide

Suicide also creates aloneness, because surrounding family and friends react with horror, guilt for failure to recognize the signals and help, and hushed silence. Talking about the child is taboo. Guilt and failure of the family is implied in the silence. Siblings are judged suspiciously, as potentials for suicide.

Because it is a God-directed duty to protect your family, parents and sisters and brothers do not allow themselves to be angry with the deceased child for taking his own life. His death is their failure, a failure to recognize the symptoms of depression and to provide the healthy nurturing the child needed. Self-incrimination and ambivalent emotions encourage the family to squelch memories and discussion of the deceased child. Unless the family consciously strives to forgive itself, each member will box in his or her feelings and create emotional scars that will slowly eat away hopes for happiness.

Chronic Illness

Having been supportive of the family during a child's long illness, most people find death of the child both a devastation and a release. Three undercurrents of feelings affect the emotions: relief that the child will no longer suffer, relief that life can return to normal, and expectation that the parents will put their sorrows to rest, since death was the anticipated climax to the illness.

The bereaved family will not accept the death of their child as easily as may be expected. Others may have realized death was the natural conclusion to the chronic illness, but rarely has the family considered death as inevitable. The illness has demanded their time, finances, and energy. Usually emotionally and physically drained, with few reserves left to deal with the reality of the pain of grief, and with the support of friends diminished, the family unit may be in serious danger.

Acute Illness and Accidents

Community support is at its greatest level when a child's death results from a sudden, unexpected health problem or accident. In the back of each parent's mind is the thought, *This could happen to one of my children.* Shock and despair become empathy and sympathy. The family is allowed an extended grieving and support period.

However, accidents that were preventable through normal "good" parenting, or were the result of self-induced alcohol or drug problems, are tinged with quiet innuendos of parental failure. Though those outside the immediate family will feel sympathetic, they are less willing to suffer grief with the family that abetted the accident. This leaves the bereaved, burdened by heavy guilt, without the strong support needed to help him forgive his real or imagined failure.

Infant Death

To most people a child is not a child until he becomes a personality; therefore, the longer a child lives, the more acceptable are parental expressions of grief. The idea of a baby being a vital part of the family from the moment of conception and worthy of grief is difficult to understand in a society that bases worth on productivity.

A short grieving period is allowed mothers of miscarried or stillborn infants, because of their sentimentality about babies; a father's emotional upset is considered a reaction to his wife's swinging emotions and the medical costs. Parents aching for the lost potential of their child find little understanding and support.

In addition to others' intolerance of the normal expressions of grief allowed for an older child, families of young infants who die experience tremendous guilt. The deaths often draw police investigation and friends' and family's suspicions of negligence. Most families bear deep emotional scars from withholding hurt after their baby's death. They feel the sting of advice to have another baby shared incondolences. "Whys," aired as people search to justify the death, sear guilt into their souls. They do not rebound quickly.

Twenty years after her infant died, a friend swelled with anger as she related the horror of returning from the hospital to find their baby's room dismantled. Thinking the baby paraphernalia would increase the parents' anguish, friends had packed and taken it away. Insensitivity abounds around those who lose an infant.

Tailor-made Grief

It would be easy to say "death is death," but it is only a half-truth. Death comes packaged in tailor-made grief. Grief is like a cake that starts with the way the child dies and blends the individual's self-esteem, relationship to the deceased child, and relationship with God. The blended ingredients in each person affect his ability to cope versus quit, to control or be controlled by his emotions, to shape or be shaped by his focus.

Certainly the pain is unbearable; no one can make it go away, but you can make it easier. As a support, express your concern and love for the bereaved without passing judgment on the rightness or wrongness of his child's death or the length of his bereavement. You can appreciate the uniqueness of each person's reaction to the death. You can offer the only real help, sharing God's love and your concern.

Focus: Key to Recovery

Focus is the key that opens the way to recovery. After a child's death, focus often centers on the anger felt at God, the villain, the cause of the accident, or self. If you stay centered on the hurt and rage, the tragedy will continue to destroy lives.

Focus must pull away from your own pain. The more you work at healing your hurt by spinning webs to mend your own anguish, the more you are wrapped. The wrappings become strong bindings that separate you from everyone else. Wallowing in self-pity drowns hope for recovery. Pity allows weaknesses, lack of responsibility, and laziness; it keeps the focus on "what could have been."

After the doctors shared with me that LeeAnne's brain had been destroyed by massive swelling, would I have chosen her death? Never! I would have spent the rest of my life nursing her body, talking to her silent form. I would have been grateful to have had her to love, no matter the cost to me. Though I would not have chosen continued "living death" for LeeAnne, I would have chosen it for me.

LeeAnne's death was easier to endure, because a virus took her life, rather than a man brutalizing and murdering her. We did not have to work through her screams, her terror at knowing someone hurt her, and not understanding why we did not come to her rescue. Yet there was nothing easy about our family's recovery.

Recovery was a choice to focus on the positive and throw away the hurt, the anger, and the questions. It was a choice to acknowledge God's control over life and death and be grateful for the life we shared with LeeAnne without wishing for the time we missed.

Stimulate healing and acceptance of tragedy by:

- Focusing on God's promise that there is a purpose in life and death.
- Focusing on the joy of the shared time with the child, the value of the life as opposed to the longevity.
- Focusing on gratitude that the child did not suffer or cope with an extremely limited longer life.
- Focusing on helping prevent other similar tragedies, through legislation and community-awareness programs.
- Focusing on helping others—family and friends—cope with the child's death in a way that will return peace and joy to their lives.

Develop a Balanced Focus

The bereaved must carefully develop their focus and avoid allowing emotions to change a potentially good focus into a destructive one. For happiness to return to our lives, negative focus must be eliminated, but positive focus must also be kept in balance.

It seems healthy to focus on the quality of life versus the longevity. Taken to an extreme, however, you could develop intolerant attitudes toward those who fall outside the "normal health" range. This out-of-control focus would reason the injustice of someone with less capabilities than your child being granted the right to live.

Having a reason for life, a "cause," can be positive. The

family can use it as a goal that makes the struggle through grief worthwhile, or the goal can debilitate the family as it consumes the precious time needed to bind the family together.

Focusing on helping others can pull you away from your own emptiness and fill the vacancy with shared joys, or it can become the escape from facing your own hurts and pains.

To be happy, you'll need balance in all areas of life, following God's principle.

Focus must not:

- Keep you too busy to deal with family relationship needs.
- Make the "cause" more important than caring and sharing of self with others, especially your family.
- Keep you from facing your own emotional needs.
- Create intolerant attitudes toward others.

"In all things give thanks" is a biblical injunction that requires great faith. It is also a key to our psychological makeup that prevents simmering emotions and bitterness. The way death comes is merely a factor; the child is gone. The justice or injustice of the death, the reactions of others, and the surrounding family crises after death must not take control of focus.

We must use the God-given secret, an attitude of thanks, to renew our sense of joy and peace. Unfortunately, thanksgiving after the death of your child requires the hardest task of the grief process: letting go!

Twelve

Never Say Die _____

Is it important to understand why our society denies death? Probably it *is* important if you are coping with your child's death.

It might help you understand why people shy away from you.
It might help you understand why no one will talk to you about your child.
It might give you insights into your husband's or wife's locked emotions.

It might allow you to free yourself from a great deal of guilt
when you are not restored to "normal" life overnight.

Perhaps you will understand why you feel so isolated.

You may find clues to help your children cope.

You may analyze what you need to do for your family to grow
closer to God and one another.

You may be able to reject some of society's wrong notions and
expectations about coping with death, notions that cause
you to bury deep emotional needs instead of dealing with
them.

A Change in Society

For thousands of years, history repeated itself: Life followed the same paths; attitudes and coping remained constant; changes occurred slowly. Traditional home and cultural
expectations helped the newborn baby develop the necessary
strong self-concept to meet the challenges of life.

Seven essential tools helped the child:

1. Self-esteem.
2. Perception of self as capable.
3. Sense of being able to control and change world.
4. Skills to negotiate, cooperate, and communicate.
5. Analytical skills for judgment.
6. Sense of being needed.
7. Feeling of responsibility for self and others.[1]

As these tools honed the child's mental and emotional
supports, he was blanketed in the necessary elements for a
strong self-image: the sense of being loved, needed, accepted,
responsible, and capable.

During the nineteenth century, the mechanical revolution,
urbanization, and industrialization joined forces to engender a
new world. The twentieth century became a world of constant
change: change in technology, change in acceptable life-
styles, change in priorities. Giving a child the tools previous

generations had considered important was no longer critical to our technically advanced society. The cost of failure of families and the education system to instill these traditional skills in the twentieth-century child has been great. Lacking maturity and coping skills, we see a new generation suffering from family instability, individual insecurity, and "me" centered attitudes.

Nine facets of today's life-style have negatively affected the ability to cope when tragedies hit:

Waiting Time for Responsibility—Unlike most cultures, our society discourages a child from shouldering responsibility. Children are expected to "grow up" before they help with the needs of their home and family. As a result young people are less mature and responsible. Delayed responsibility develops a sense of not being needed in the child.

Anonymity—The natural support systems around a family— grandmothers, grandfathers, aunts, uncles, and cousins— have been pulled away. The average child does not know the neighbors three houses away in any direction. The typical American family moves fourteen times, a major move every four years. It becomes ingrained in the child that he is alone. His actions matter only to himself.[2]

Lack of Natural Consequences—Children rarely experience the natural consequences of their actions; parents try to prevent negative experiences. Therefore, a child does not recognize that actions bring reactions. He feels as if fate and luck are in control.

Education Is All-important—To be a success, you must do well academically. In previous generations, if a child were not good in school, he or she could achieve success in other areas of life, like building fences or sewing clothes. Today self-esteem is won or lost in the classroom. The child learns that self-value is based upon performance, as judged by others.

Over-protection—In an effort to protect our children from hurts, we tell them what to do, how to do it, and when to do it.

This spoon-feeding cuts down on failures, but it creates little training in judgment, cooperation, and negotiation, necessary skills for mature decision making.

Expanded Arena—Children are besieged with news of problems throughout the world: hunger, strikes, wars, death, and disease. The endless chaos of world needs creates a feeling of helplessness. There is too much to be done, so why do anything? The lesson learned early by the child is that he is too limited to make a difference.

Weakened Family—With both parents working, divorce, split families, television, and rare home responsibilities, children grow up feeling isolated and independent. They are not trained in communication and negotiation. They don't feel essential to the family, nor does the family seem essential to them.

Instant and Throwaway Society—If it doesn't work, throw it away! If it can't be obtained instantly, forget it! Children grow up expecting easy solutions.

Constant Entertainment—Life is to be enjoyed. Problems take away from the fun; therefore, do not deal with them, and perhaps they will go away. Our children are taught to fill their time with activities, leaving no time to resolve the normal problems of life. Delayed gratification is part of the past.

A society that does not like to deal with problems, wants to feel good instantly, has not learned to communicate, and builds self-esteem on externals will find it hard to handle death. When we do not feel needed, loved, accepted, capable of handling our life, and responsible for our actions, the ups and downs of life are overwhelming. Death is a down that we try to wish away. Untrained to deal with long-term problems and lacking the skills to communicate, you and your family are left on shaky ground.

The only way to survive as an individual, as a couple, and as a family is to plan your strategy. Force yourself to use reason to guide your family through the difficult times. How?

- By being concerned for the welfare of others—your spouse, children, extended family and friends.
- By being open about your feelings.
- By asking for and accepting help.
- By communicating so that walls of misunderstanding do not form.
- By resolving each problem as you confront it, not pushing it aside, hoping it will go away.
- By accepting the responsibility for your family's healthy emotional survival.
- By accepting the consequences of the choices you make.
- By trusting that with God's help you and your family can survive.

We must deal with the attitudes our society teaches, but we do not have to be bound by them. With God's help, we can walk through the emotional mire of death and develop the skills that will build our family's closeness. The outcome will be a growth that will help us meet life's challenges and a confidence in our strength through God.

Thirteen

Reconciling Tragedy With Blessing ——————

The death of my child has been the deepest tragedy of my life. The death of my child has brought the most difficult challenge to my survival. From surviving the death of my child have come the greatest blessings of my life.

Letting go does not mean erasing the memories and love of your child. Letting go is a release of the pain and yearning. It is the end, not the beginning, the end of a long, painful growing and healing process.

From the moment of our child's death, we fought to hold

on to LeeAnne. Death had denied the physical grasp, but it could not take away the emotional clutch. We idealized our child, dwelled on the memories, yearned for her, and burdened ourselves with guilt if we allowed the slightest bit of happiness to creep into our corner of depression.

We had to choose to let go. It does not just happen; it is a struggle. I remember—with aching—the moment I released LeeAnne. A year and a half had passed since her death. I had continued to live. My life revolved around surviving and helping my family survive together. Walking by reason, not my emotions, I forced myself to go, to move, to be involved. When my emotions threatened to pull me under, I would leave the house—jog, do Nautilus, swim, or visit a friend. I involved myself in many teaching activities in the church and community. Teaching gave me the impetus to stay positive.

Continuing life, acting positive, is simply the first step that allows you to take control of your emotions and to begin the walk to healing. Inside, the emotions still beg to lead. Fighting with reason, they scream, "How can you forget?" "Do you remember . . . ?" "You can't stop hurting. It would be disloyal." Whenever you see another child, they hurl remembrances. Anything can bring back painful thoughts and tears—waiting in a nursery-school line for your younger child, seeing an old friend, reading a book that was special to her. The list is as varied as her life.

> The hours, not moment, I released LeeAnne were anguishing. I was on an Emmaus Walk, a religious weekend retreat. I had chosen to go, but in my emotions, I wondered if God deserved my attention. My inner spiritual battle peaked, "God, if You took my little girl, if You let her die, then take away my pain. It isn't fair. I've done everything I can to walk in trust—yet I hurt so deeply. You can have LeeAnne, but I can't stand the pain."
>
> In my mind, I begged. I pleaded. I cried. I screamed. I wailed in anguish. *I want my baby. You shouldn't have*

taken her away. She was mine. I was doing a good job with her. It isn't fair! Why? Why would You take my greatest treasure? My children are mine. Why? The crust broke. The anger I had denied ended.

I made the *choice*. I spoke the truth. I quit denying the hurt. It had not been all right with me for God to take LeeAnne, and I finally admitted it. At the same moment I realized an even more important point for my life: *I can live without wealth. I can live without my husband. I can live without my children. But I cannot live without God.*

Grow? Grow from this horror? Yes. Losing my little girl has been the greatest tragedy of my life. LeeAnne's death was a devastation! My reaction could have become the second tragedy, causing the destruction of the rest of my family. With LeeAnne's death have come the most difficult challenges of my life. From the tragedy and surviving the tragedy have also come the greatest blessings.

Letting go was so difficult that I was nonfunctional for a week after the choice. My energy was completely gone. My emotions were flat. I was drained. But I was at peace.

Reaching for Blessings

Before you can receive healing and blessing, you must choose to let go.

Steps to Letting Go

1. You must move through the healing process of grief.
2. Deal with your emotions honestly. You cannot let go of a child without hurt—no matter how great your faith or trust. Face that hurt and release it.
3. You must confront the reality that life without God is empty.
4. You must turn your life's controls over to God. Through

trust and acceptance, you can handle whatever happens in life's journey.

Emotions Changing to Blessings

Whirling emotions *can* change to blessings. Emotional whammies can change to blessings in grief—if you trust God's direction.

Five emotions battle for control after tragedy.

I'm different!   The thought reverberates through every activity and throws blankets of insecurity and isolation around you.

With healing, "I'm different" changes to "I am God's!" The attitude becomes wrapped in peace, "With God, I can safely journey through any walk in life."

I'm crazy!   The inability to think straight, to remember, to focus is a blessing. Being "crazy" keeps the full thrust of tragedy at bay. The force of hurt hits in small doses. Numbness and confusion block the full impact. In gradual steps that allow acceptance, reality becomes clear.

I'm in pain!   Only those who have walked through a deep tragedy can understand the depth of anguish. Out of the experience of such hurt comes a blessing—a caring spirit. You receive the ability to empathize, to feel the hurt of others as one who has been there. Life takes on deeper meaning.

I'm bad!   Throughout most of life we center our evaluations on how we have been wronged by others. When deep tragedy hits, the reflection and reevaluation of life centers on self: "What could I have done differently?"

Insights, coupled with forgiveness, turn the suffering of guilt into a gift. Nothing equals the hurt from the tragedy. Therefore, there is sadness for the missed opportunities of the past, but not despair. Empathy builds understanding that allows you to forgive others. More important, it allows you to forgive yourself!

I can't. The feelings that bind you from reaching out to others for help, that keep you focused on yourself, change. The focus changes to "I can do anything with God's help!"

Fear of tragedy, failure, the ups and downs of life are gone. Though life will always be fluid, always changing, our rebellious attitude toward the problems of life changes to acceptance of them as hurdles to overcome with God's guidance.

Two Spiritual Truths

As you allow God to direct your choices after tragedy, two unfolding spiritual understandings unite your fighting mind and emotions. The first is that God's Spirit dwells within you. Watching reason win the battle over your runaway emotions, the realization dawns that God is in you, a part of your spirit. Choosing to follow God's leading, you gradually control your grief; without His guidance you flounder in the seas of despair.

The second understanding is that with God in you, the difficulties of life are hurdles, not walls. Tragedies become challenges that build, as opposed to blocks that stymie you. Experiencing the power of your spirit to lead grants a sense of spiritual oneness with God. You fill with the quiet peace that passeth understanding, spoken of in Philippians 4:7. The vacuum of emptiness, which is a by-product of anger against God, for allowing such hardships, changes to peace as you trust Him with all parts of your life.

We are offered the choice between two gift-wrapped packages with grief: one filled with bitterness and anger, one filled with blessings. Both gifts change your life. Pray that you make the right choice!

The Choice for Survival

Letting go. Choosing survival after LeeAnne's death was the most difficult challenge of my life. It took great effort, but we made it as a family. LeeAnne will always be a vital part of our lives. Tears will well in my eyes forever when I think of the blessings her life brought us.

The years since her death have been filled with challenge and choice. It has not been easy! The shadows have slowly been replaced by rainbows.

Still, I miss that little girl!

Appendix I

A Guide to Funeral Services and Planning _____

Our European ancestors ritualized death into recognizable customs: death clothes, horse-drawn death carriages, year-long wearing of black, wakes, and flamboyant burial services. Though we have seen, perhaps participated in many of these customs, our American funeral rites today are far more simplified.

The Services

There are three services in our Christian American tradition: the visitation, funeral service, and graveside service.

(This is rapidly changing to a one-service rite held in the funeral building.) Visitation generally takes place two days after the death; the funeral and cemetery services follow the next day.

The Visitation

One hundred years ago the visitation took place in the home. The visitation was a "wake" as friends and family visited, watching over the body, talking, "sitting" with the deceased until "his soul left." The soul was thought to remain earthbound for twenty-four hours, after which the deceased was buried in his "going-away clothes" and a handmade death blanket, quilted from strips of old family clothing.

Today the visitation has become a formalized time. Friends and acquaintances visit during a set time on the second day after death, usually at a "parlor" in the funeral home. Visitors greet the family, expressing condolences, hugging, and shaking hands. Often family members will be tranquilized by drugs. The contrast to the wake's informality, in the home, a hundred years ago, where emotional outcries were acceptable, is significant.

The wake began a healing process as family and friends talked and cried through their feelings and shared memories. Today's visitation usually grants family and friends a feeling of support, but does not allow time for the relaxed, critical sharing. The wake focused on the interplay of the deceased's life with those around him. The focus of the visitation is on the loss.

To return an element of sharing to the visitation, you may wish to do as we did and have it in your home.

The Funeral Service

The funeral service is traditionally held the third day after the death, symbolic of Christ's arising from the dead. Generally this service is held in the family's church or a funeral home and enables the pastor to give the family some spiritual support. Outside of such a service, many of us rarely have any teaching on death.

Graveside Service

Traditionally, following the funeral service, friends and family travel via caravan to the gravesite. The full reality of the child's death hits at this time, and families leave devastated. This is why we changed the order of services, placing LeeAnne's graveside service before the funeral service. We felt that allowed the friends and family to leave the last rite on a more positive note.

Funeral Plans

If you are dealing with the possibility—or the actuality—of your child's death, make plans. Don't let it just happen. The funeral rites are the initiation into grief, not the end of the grieving process.

The initiation has the potential to be uplifting, beginning a positive progression, or you can be thrown into a crypt by services that tear your thin layer of emotional stability to shreds.

Your emotions scream out the need for the services to let the world know the tragedy of your loss. Never was there another child like this one, and you want the services to be a fitting celebration of your child's life. You are vaguely aware of the importance the services will have in your memory banks as the weeks, months, and years pass. How can you insure a positive farewell?

Keep three thoughts in mind:

1. You want to do whatever will be best for your family's emotional health.
2. The rules of the rites are not set in concrete.
3. The final choices for the services are *yours*.

Services do not have to be elaborate to be lovely. No ornamentation or trimmings will make a service special. A service that leaves the congregation with appreciation for the deceased and knowledge that God is the chief source of comfort in all situations will be centered on the top priority— helping you gain strength to face the days ahead.

Special Touches

Flowers versus memorials.   When a child dies, the family will receive many floral arrangements, no matter what they request. Alternatively they may start a memorial fund, which provides a tangible way for friends and family to show their concern. It gives the family money with which to perpetuate the child's memory.

Memorials are usually handled by a church, though they can be directed to a bank or the family. The church or bank puts the funds into a separate account. Partial or total funds can be withdrawn by the family, whenever desired. No accounting is required by the fund-holding institution. The funds draw interest at the current bank rate in both the church and bank. Funds given through the church memorials can be a tax-deductible donation to the giver. Notification of all memorial gifts is sent to the family.

Open versus closed caskets.   Open caskets are an American custom. The merits of viewing the deceased should be considered:

1.   Psychologists who support the idea say viewing the body helps the family and friends accept the reality of death.
2.   Psychologists against it contend that viewing the body and offering typical comments like "Doesn't she look pretty?" indicate a strong denial of death.

3. According to the FDA, "viewing" the body is the cornerstone of the funeral industry, requiring padded caskets, restoration, and embalming.
4. The funeral business argues that since the body is housed in the funeral home, viewing allows more time to "adjust" to the death.

Yours is the final decision.

Timing. Timing is an important choice that affects who can attend the services; you must carefully choose the timing. If you want friends of the deceased youth to attend, set the funeral service after school hours.

Music. The music was one of the greatest contributing factors to our sense of peace in LeeAnne's services. Music is able to soothe and minister, calming the spirit.

Costs

The funeral industry is a $6.4 billion a year business. The costs of a typical service will vary from $3,000 to over $30,000, according to the services rendered and the type of funerary purchased. Though the United States Department of Commerce has projected that funeral costs will rise almost 9 percent each year in the next decade, competition has actually caused a slight decline in prices since the late 1970s.[1]

I am not about to contend that Americans are getting ripped off at our friendly neighborhood funeral homes. Unquestionably, funeral-home directors meet a social need. But theirs is a business, not a social service. Their time, like that of all professionals, is as important as the material goods they offer for sale.

Funeral directors offer financial counseling and help with travel plans, if the body is to be buried elsewhere. They also coordinate schedules, write the obituary, make arrangements for the rites, care for the deceased body, and provide services to meet individual needs. They must maintain expensive vehicles, pay off mortgages, utilities, operating expenses, and a twenty-four-hour staff.

After five years of hearings, in mid-June 1978, the Federal Trade Commission released a 526-page report on the funeral industry. Six major factors, they concluded, handicap the bargaining position of the funeral purchaser: the emotional trauma, guilt, dependence, suggestibility, ignorance, and time pressure. Inborn anger can grow in the consumer, because he has no time to make the choices—and he didn't want the death anyway!

Choices in the Funeral Home

Funeral home.   Funerals are not by law mandated to be handled by morticians in funeral homes. It is possible to bury an individual in a private site, without embalming or casket. For most, however, the option is not a consideration.

Funeral homes differ in services rendered, costs of services, and types and cost of caskets. Most often the choice of which mortuary to employ is based on a suggestion, the type of structure, and gut reaction. When your child dies, you will not want to comparison shop for cost. But if you have definite desires for unusual types of services, check the possibilities with the director before committing to his funeral home.

Embalming.   The first service of the mortician is to secure the body from the hospital or home. Unless directed otherwise, he will embalm the body. Embalming is the replacing of the body fluids with a formalin solution. A body begins to decay from internal bacteria within twenty-four hours after death, and the formalin solution slows down the inevitable breakdown.

Though it is customary procedure to embalm, most states do not require it. If the services are within two days, the body can be refrigerated. This is appropriate for immediate closed-casket services or cremation. Some families object to the procedure of embalming, others to the additional cost.

Clothing. Involve brothers and sisters. Let them choose a special article to leave with their sibling—a doll, a stuffed animal, or a book. We took LeeAnne's Cabbage Patch doll with the big red pigtails and a Tenderheart Care Bear to snuggle with her. A friend brought an angel, which we had placed on top of the casket in the vault.

Casket. In bygone days a wooden coffin was made by the local carpenter or a family member. Coffins came in all shapes and sizes, with such picturesque names as *squeezin' casket, toothpicked toe, bent corner,* and *toe pincher.* The rectangular coffin dates from the 1860s. Usually coffins were lined with homespun or velvet and ranged in cost from ten to twenty-five dollars.

As we became more urban, furniture makers made and sold caskets. Sears was a purveyor of coffins, advertising that their specialties ranged from the beginning to end of life. Today we purchase a casket from the funeral director's display room. The price varies from $300 to more than $15,000, depending upon the casket's cushioning, corrosion guard, ventilation, lightning-proof quality, or degree of elaborate encasing.

Small caskets are not in great demand. Knowing that funeral homes can order others from catalogs, available through overnight shipping, may be a relief if you are unhappy with the selection or cost.

Two other options should be considered as possibilities when considering the type of casket:

> Pall—A heavy cloth—usually black, gray, purple, or burgundy—that drapes the coffin, it is often available free of charge to church members and for a nominal fee to others. Available for rent or purchase through a funeral home,

purchased palls can be used as a traditional family cover. Used often over a wooden coffin.

Blanket of flowers—Upon request a florist will provide a cascade of flowers that drapes the casket.

Vault. A vault is a cement or steel encasement for the casket. Though it is not a legal requirement to purchase a vault, most mortuary grounds require that the casket be lowered into one. While protecting the casket, the vault also keeps the ground from sinking. This is a good place to save hundreds of dollars.

Choices at the Memorial Park

Choosing the cemetery. The memorial park provides perpetual care, monument options, insurance to protect monuments against theft, professional grave diggers, and staff to set the monuments.

Just as there are rules and regulations for use of the funeral home or church, each private or public cemetery has regulations that govern everything from the size of the plot to type of monuments allowed. Type of burial (mausoleum, columbarium niches, ash gardens, or in-ground) must be decided before you can choose the necessary burial equipment—vault, urn, or casket.

Markers. There are four types of markers: monuments, footstones, headstones, and cornerstones. Prices for markers and monuments vary substantially for the same product. Sandblasting and laser techniques make it possible to reproduce any two-dimensional design on the marker. Selecting, personalizing, and purchasing a marker may take months. Because it is such a huge undertaking, many families have another service at the time of its placement.

Personalizing your child's stone may give you a sense of creating a special tribute to him. Whatever evokes happy thoughts of his life—trains, a favorite toy, or a picture—may be helpful to your family. Our favorite picture of LeeAnne, with the addition of angel wings, was sandblasted into the marker. It is LeeAnne's stone. There will never be another one like it. Like LeeAnne, the stone is unique.

It is fun to peruse the tombstones in old cemeteries. Many tell a small history of the life, involving the reader in the realization that a person with feelings and emotions was buried beneath the ground. The Williamsburg Episcopal Church cemetery is filled with markers that bring alive a time. In Philadelphia's Christ Church Cemetery, one can read Ben Franklin's epitaph:

> *The body of*
> *Benjamin Franklin Printer,*
> *(Like the cover of an old book*
> *Its Contents torn out*
> *And stript of its lettering and gilding)*
> *Lies here, food for worms;*
> *But the work shall not be lost,*
> *For it will, (as he believed) appear*
> *once more*
> *In a new and more elegant edition*
> *Revised and corrected*
> *By the author.*

Appendix II

Special Helps

Writing thank-you notes was horrible. We were grateful for friends and family, and all their special remembrances touched and uplifted our whole family. But sitting down, saying, "Thank-you," was dreadful. Why? Because it was tragic. Every letter reminded us that LeeAnne was dead. This was real, not a dream from which I would awaken.

Help came in the mail. Learning LeeAnne had died, a college friend sent us the thank-you note she had designed when her eight-year-old son died from leukemia. The note

We appreciate so much your prayers and expressions of sympathy extended during our loss of LeeAnne.

Even though our hearts are heavy and our family seems incomplete, having friends and relatives caring and helping has been more support than it is possible to convey.

It is simply too painful to write each person individually, but please know we have read, reread, studied and taken comfort from every card, flower, gift, food, telephone call and visit.

God sends friends as a blessing in times like these. They are the plus that helps pull you through the sorrow. Thank you for your part in helping us deal with our separation from Lee.

With love,
Paul, Betty, Kim, Paul, Brad

Brown Oaks Manor
1911 Triangle Road
Johnson City, Tenn.

was a beautiful way to say, "Thank you." In stick figures she had drawn her family at the top of the card. The message thanked everyone for the many ways they had upheld her family. It was perfect.

Above is our thank-you note. Stick figures on the note's top represented our family. The stick figure on the envelope was LeeAnne. The message was handwritten in black felt-tip pen, without the giver's name. Our local printer printed the eight-and-a-half-by-five-and-a-half-inch notecards on standard card stock. The person's name was then written on the notecard and envelope with the same felt-tip pen. The cards were personal and special. What a help!

Books

With adults and children who are working through grief, books are a wonderful tool. Listed below are a few of my favorites:

For Children

Buscaglia, Leo. *The Fall of Freddie the Leaf.* New York: Henry Holt & Co., 1982.

Dodge, Nancy C. *Thumpy's Story.* Springfield, Ill.: Prairie Lark, 1985.

Mellonie, Bryan and Robert Ingpen. *Lifetimes.* New York: Bantam Books, 1983.

Kübler-Ross, Elisabeth. *Remember the Secret.* Millbrae, Ca.: Celestial Arts, 1981.

Viorst, Judith. *The Tenth Good Thing About Barney*. New York: Atheneum, 1971.

For Adults

Bardow, Joan. *The Ultimate Loss: Coping With the Death of a Child*. New York: Beaufort Books, 1982.

Briggs, Lauren Littauer. *What You Can Say When You Don't Know What to Say*. Eugene, Ore.: Harvest House, 1985.

Buckingham, Robert W. *A Special Kind of Love—Care of the Dying Child*. New York: Continuum Pub. Co., 1984.

Graham, Billy. *Facing Death and the Life After*. Waco, Tex.: Word Books, 1987.

Kübler-Ross, Elisabeth. *On Death and Dying*. New York: Macmillan Pubs., 1969.

Landorf, Joyce. *Mourning Song*. Old Tappan, N.J.: Fleming H. Revell Co., 1974.

Lewis, C. S. *A Grief Observed*. New York: Harper & Row, 1963.

Rando, Theresa A. *Grief, Dying and Death*. Champaign, Ill.: Research Press Co., 1984.

Vail, Elaine. *A Personal Guide to Living With Loss*. New York: John Wiley & Sons, 1982.

Westberg, Granger E. *Good Grief*. Philadelphia: Fortress Press, 1962.

Organizations

There are support groups for most types of death that claim children: death by accident, disease, abuse, murder, Sudden Infant Death Syndrome, cancers, perinatal and neonatal problems. Each group focuses on support. If your area does not have a local chapter, the national organization will gladly send you brochures, with guides for coping and sources of help.

This listing includes only the largest of the support-outreach groups working with bereaved families in the loss of a child. Check with the personnel director of your community hospital or churches for listing of local support organizations.

Compassionate Friends, Inc.
P.O. Box 1347
Oak Brook, IL 60521
(312) 323-5010
Over 500 chapters throughout the country help bereaved families deal with the loss of their child.

Grief Education Institute
2422 S. Downing Street
Denver CO 80210
(303) 777-9234
Through national organizations and local chapters, provides support services to the general public and to professionals.

Hospice
1901 North Fort Myer Drive
Arlington, VA 22209
(703) 243-5900
Support to patient and family, through volunteers and related professional services—emotional support, physical care, transportation—total support package.

MADD—Mothers Against Drunk Driving
669 Airport Freeway
Suite 310
Hurst, TX 76053
National organization with local chapters for support of bereaved family after the loss of a child in a drunk-driving accident. Organized effort to lobby for legislation against drunk driving and to educate the public about the problem.

Parents of Murdered Children
1739 Bella Vista
Cincinnati, OH 45237
(513) 242-5683
Special help for the bereaved who must deal with the horror of their child's murder.

Ray of Hope
1518 Derwen Drive
Iowa City, IA 52240
Local chapters throughout the states, to uphold families and friends of suicide victims.

Ronald McDonald Houses
1 Ronald Lane
Oakbrook, IL 60601
(312) 575-3400
Home provided for family use during child's hospitalizations.

Share
St. John's Hospital
800 East Carpenter
Springfield, IL 62769
(217) 544-6464
Over 120 groups primarily support parents of newborns who die as a result of miscarriage, ectopic pregnancy, stillbirth, or after-birth complications.

S.I.D.S.
P.O. Box 2357
Landover Hills, MD 20784
1-800-221-S.I.D.S. or 301-459-3388
National organization with local chapters to support research and bereaved from Sudden Infant Death syndrome.

Source Notes

Chapter 1

1. Katherine Fair Donnelly, *Recovering From the Loss of a Child* (New York: Macmillan Pubs., 1982), 44.

2. *Facts About Sudden Infant Death Syndrome*, (Landover, Md.: National Sudden Infant Death Syndrome Foundation, 1979), 1.

3. U.S. Department of Commerce, *Statistical Abstract of the U.S.*, 107th ed. (Washington, D.C.: U.S. Government Printing Office, 1987), 63.

4. National Center for Health Statistics, *Monthly Vital Statistics, Trends and Deathrates by Age*, Supplement 5, Vol. 36 (August 28, 1987), 161.

5. Donnelly, *Recovering* , 22.

6. Donald Langsley and David M. Kaplan, *The Treatment of Families in Crisis* (New York: Grune Pubs., 1968).

Chapter 2

1. Elisabeth Kübler-Ross, *On Death and Dying* (New York, Macmillan Pub., 1969), 38–137.

2. Charles V. Gerkin, *Crisis Experience in Modern Life* (Nashville, Tenn.: Abingdon Press, 1979), 154–166.

3. John Bowlby and Murray Parkes, *Normal and Pathological Responses to Bereavement*, ed. John Ellard (New York: MSS Information Corp., 1974), 232ff.

Chapter 3

1. Kenneth L. Carder, Coping With Loss and Grief Seminar (Athens, Tenn.: Hiwassee College, 1986).

Chapter 4

1. Lesley Weatherhead, *The Will of God* (Nashville, Tenn.: Abingdon Press, 1976), 20.

Chapter 5

1. Erich Lindeman, *American Journal of Psychiatry*, Vol. 101 (September 1944), 141–148. Erich Lindeman, *Beyond Grief* (New York: Jason Aronson, Inc., 1979).

2. Elisabeth Kübler-Ross, interview with Rev. Kenneth L. Carder, Knoxville, Tenn., 1978.

3. John Richman, *A General Selection From the Works of Sigmund Freud* (New York: Liveright Publ., 1987), 80.

4. Bill Gillham, *Lifetime Guarantee* (Brentwood, Ind.: Wolgamuth & Hyatt Pub., 1987, 123–135.

Chapter 7

1. William G. Justice, *When Death Comes* (Nashville, Tenn.: Broadman Press, 1982), 75.

Chapter 8

1. Elaine Vail, *A Personal Guide to Living With Loss* (New York: John Wiley & Sons, 1982), 67.

2. Ira O. Glick, Murray C. Parkes, Robert S. Weiss, *The First Year of Bereavement* (New York: John Wiley & Sons, 1974), 55.

Chapter 9

1. Dr. James A. Mercy, Center for Disease Control, Intentional Injury Section, Atlanta, Georgia, September 29, 1987.

2. Ibid.

3. U.S. Department of Commerce, *Statistical Abstract of the U.S.*, 107th ed. (Washington, D.C.: U.S. Gov't Printing Office, 1987), 79.

4. Center for Disease Control, Division of Injury Epidemiology and Control, *Homicide Surveillance* (Atlanta. U.S. Department of Health and Human Services, 1987), 15.

5. Julie Lays, "Too Young to Die," *National Conference of State Legislatures*, November/December (Washington, D.C.: State Legislatures Publication, 1986), 18.

6. "Suicide in America," *Miami News* (August 30, 1982), B–1.

7. Department of Commerce, *Statistical Abstract*, 76.

8. Center for Disease Control, Violence Epidemiology Branch, *Youth Suicide Surveillance* (Atlanta: U.S. Department of Health and Human Services), 4.

9. Ibid.

10. Ibid., 22.

11. Center for Disease Control, Violence Epidemiology Branch, *Suicide Surveillance* (Atlanta: U.S. Department of Health and Human Services), 4.

12. "Suicide in America," B–1.

13. Debbie Porterfield, "Special Report on Suicide," *Tampa Tribune* (October 7, 1984), 1.

14. Ibid.

15. Ibid.

16. Elaine Vail, *A Personal Guide to Living With Loss* (New York: John Wiley & Sons, 1982), 166.

17. Center for Disease Control, *Youth Suicide Surveillance*, 6.

18. Ed Magnuson, "The Curse of Violent Crime," *Time* (March 23, 1981), 16.

19. Department of Commerce, *Statistical Abstract*, 75.

20. Gary Turbak, "Missing," *Kiwanis Magazine* (1982), 22.

21. Center for Disease Control, *Homicide Surveillance*, 5.

22. Ibid.

23. Carol J. R. Hogue, James W. Buehler, Lilo T. Strauss, Jack C. Smith, "Overview of the National Infant Mortality Surveillance (NIMS) Project—Design, Methods, Results," *Public Health Reports*, Vol. 102 (Washington, D.C.: U.S. Department of Health and Human Services, 1987) 2:126.

24. David P. Roe, Medical Center OB-GYN Practice, Johnson City, Tn., October 2, 1987.

25. C. George Ray, Abraham B. Bergman, J. Bruce Beckwith, "An Analysis of the Problem," *Pediatric Annals* (November, 1974), 6.

26. Ibid., 10–11.

27. Dr. James A. Mercy, ibid.

Chapter 10

1. William G. Justice, *When Death Comes* (Nashville, Tn.: Broadman Press, 1982), 67.

Chapter 12

1. Steve Glenn, "Families in Transition," Talk recorded on South Carolina Educational Radio Network (Columbia, South Carolina: Staff Development of S.C. Educational Radio Network, 1985).

2. Celia Boertlein, "The Geographic Mobility of America," *American Movers Conference Journal* (October, 1985), 11.

Appendix I

1. Jean Rosenblatt, "Funeral Business Under Fire," *Editorial Research Reports*, Vol. 11, 2:815–816.

Bibliography

Briggs, Lauren. *What You Can Say When You Don't Know What to Say.* Eugene, Ore.: Harvest House Pub., 1982.

Bachman, D. Charles. *Ministering to the Grief Sufferers.* New York: Prentice-Hall, 1964.

Bardow, Joan. *The Ultimate Loss: Coping With the Death of a Child.* New York: Beaufort Books, 1982.

Boertlein, Celia. "The Geographic Mobility of Americans." *American Movers Conference Journal.* (October 1985).

Bowlby, John and Murray Parkes. *Normal and Pathological Responses to Bereavement*, ed. John Ellard. New York: MSS Information, 1974.

Buckingham, Robert. *A Special Kind of Love—Care of the Dying Child.* New York: Continuum Press, 1983.

Carder, Kenneth L. *Coping With Loss and Grief* Seminar. Athens, Tenn.: Hiwassee College, 1986.

Donnelly, Katherine Fair. *Recovering From the Loss of a Child.* New York: Macmillan Pub., 1982.

Gannett, Lewis. *Family Book of Verse.* New York: Harper & Bros., 1961.

Gerkin, Charles V. *Crisis Experience in Modern Life.* Nashville, Tenn.: Abingdon Press, 1979.

Glick, Ira O., C. Murray Parkes, and Robert S. Weiss. *The First Year of Bereavement.* New York: John Wiley & Sons, 1974.

Gorer, Geoffrey. *Death, Grief, and Mourning.* New York: Doubleday, 1965.

Gillham, Bill. *Lifetime Guarantee.* Brentwood, Tenn.: Wolgemuth & Hyatt, Pub., 1987.

Hogue, Carol J. R. et al. "Overview of the National Infant Mortality Surveillance (NIMS) Project—Design, Methods, Results." *Public Health Reports,* vol. 102, no. 2 (1987).

Houk, Vernon N. *Youth Suicide.* Atlanta, Ga.: U.S. Department of Health and Human Services, 1986.

Jackson, Edgar N. *The Many Faces of Grief.* Nashville, Tenn.: Abingdon Press, 1972.

Jewett, Claudia L. *Helping Children Cope With Separation and Loss.* Cambridge, Mass.: Harvard Common Press, 1982.

Justice, William G. *When Death Comes.* Nashville, Tenn.: Broadman Press, 1982.

Kübler-Ross, Elisabeth. *Working It Through.* New York: Macmillan Pub., 1982.

————. *On Death and Dying.* New York: Macmillan Pub., 1969.

————. *On Children and Death,* New York: Macmillan Pub., 1983.

Landorf, Joyce. *Mourning Song.* Old Tappan, New Jersey: Fleming H. Revell, 1974.

Langsley, Donald and David M. Kaplan. *The Treatment of Families in Crisis.* New York: Grune Pub., 1968.

Lindemann, Erich. *Beyond Grief.* New York: Jason Aronson, 1979.

————. *American Journal of Psychiatry,* 101 (September, 1944).

Lays, Julie. "Too Young to Die." *National Conference of State Legislatures* (November/December), 1986.

Magnuson, Ed. "The Curse of Violent Crime." *Time* (March 23, 1981).

Monthly Vital Statistics, Trends, and Deathrates by Age. Vol. 36, Washington D.C.: U.S. Government Printing Office, 1987.

National Criminal Justice Information and Statistics, Washington, D.C.: U.S. Government Printing Office.

Phipps, Joyce. *Death's Single Privacy.* New York: Seabury Press, 1974.

Porterfield, Debbie. "Special Report on Suicide." *Tampa Tribune* (October 7, 1984).

Ray, C. George, Abraham B. Bergman, and J. Bruce Beckwith. "An Analysis of the Problem." *Pediatric Annals* (November, 1974).

Rickman, John, ed., and Brennar, Charles, appendix. *A General Selection From the Works of Sigmund Freud.* New York: Liveright Publ., 1957.

Rosenblatt, Jean. "Funeral Business Under Fire." *Congressional Quarterly.* Editorial Research Reports, vol. 11, no. 17 (1982).

_____. *Suicide Surveillance.* Atlanta: U.S. Department of Health and Human Services, 1985.

Schaefer, Dan and Christine Lyons, *How Do We Tell the Children?* New York: New Market Press, 1986.

Schiff, Harriet Sarnoff. *The Bereaved Parent.* New York: Crown Publ., 1977.

"Suicide in America." *Miami News* (August 30, 1982).

Tolsma, Dennis D. *Homicide Surveillance.* Atlanta, Ga.: U.S. Department of Health and Human Services, 1987.

Turbak, Gary. "Missing." *Kiwanis Magazine*, 1982.

U.S. Department of Commerce, *Statistical Abstract of the U.S. 1987*, 107th ed., Washington, D.C.: U.S. Government Printing Office, 1987.

Vail, Elaine. *A Personal Guide to Living With Loss.* New York: John Wiley & Sons, 1982.

Weatherhead, Lesley. *The Will of God*. Nashville, Tenn.: Abingdon Press, 1976.

Westburg, Granger E. *Good Grief*. Rock Island, Ill.: Augustana Books Concern, 1961.

World Health Demographic Yearbook. 37th ed., New York: U.N. Department of International Economic and Social Affairs Statistical Office, 1987.